# ONCE UPON A DREAM

## The Writer's Mind

Edited By Lynsey Evans

# THE CREATIVE WRITING

# My Mythical World

As I fall asleep, a whole new world opens just for me in my dreams.
A place I can be,
A place I can be whatever I want to be.
An amazing, mythical world full of wonder and adventure.

Aliens soar through a crystal-blue sky,
Smiling and waving as they whoosh on by.

Giant, fluffy monsters dance elegantly in the starry night,
As I joust playfully with an army of jelly knights.

The sound of dragons roaring as they bellow crimson flames,
Slowly dims into sounds of birds freely playing games.

As the sun sets in my fantastic make-believe,
I wave goodbye to a land with friends I'm never quite ready to leave.

**Blake Talbot (10)**
Cheddar Grove Primary School, Bedminster Down

# Singing Wizard

I snuggle down in my cosy bed,
I close my eyes and rest my head,
I drift off to another place,
When suddenly I see his face!
He flew into the air,
Without a care,
And sang this little song,
"I am the wizard, and my hair is long,
Wiggly worms are too,
The sky is nice and blue today! Is that a sign for you?
Down by the river, down by the bay, where my magical unicorns lay,
Maybe I'll have a wander in the deep, dark wood,
To see the fairies that are bad and good,
They might teach me a spell or two,
And how to make a secret brew!"
Then I wake up, and I'm back in my room,
I hope I get to see the wizard again soon,
But until then, I'll just look at the moon.

**Winnie Downs (10)**
Cheddar Grove Primary School, Bedminster Down

# Once Upon A Moonlit Path

Once upon a moonlit path,
Where I like to go,
I escape my home,
And trudge through the snow.
I run through fields of daisies,
And jump across small stones,
On a moonlit path, where I like to go,
I meet mermaids.
We sing and run,
But when all is said and done,
And I have had my fun,
Sadly, I have to go,
So, I...
Say goodbye to my mermaid friends,
And jump back across small stones,
On a moonlit path, where I like to go,
I run back through fields of daisies,
And drift back to bed,
I think about what was my dream,
Oh well, I can't remember, besides now I'm out of bed!

**Phoebe Castillo (10)**
Cheddar Grove Primary School, Bedminster Down

# You Are Better Than You Think

I rested my head on my pillow and wrapped myself in blankets,
But in a misty silence,
I see in the corner,
A clown chasing me,
I run into a ditch,
And close my innocent eyes,
When suddenly, I hear crying,
Oh, who could it be?
But the clown I've been dreading,
But why?
A song of words danced in my head,
"I'm not good enough,"
"To be a clown, I shouldn't be,"
I reply in a faint,
"Oh don't give up,"
"This could be your breaking point or something better!"
She smiles at me and gives me a hug,
And soon enough, I'm back at home.

**Avanna Brown (10)**
Cheddar Grove Primary School, Bedminster Down

# The Dream Jars

In a faraway place, which has been forbidden,
Something extraordinary is kept hidden.
In this magical cave, which glows and gleams,
There are rows and rows of jars containing dreams.
Some dreams are happy, cheerful and glad,
Others are depressing and lonely and sad.
Some are full of silver and treasure and gold,
Some are full of secrets, never to be told.
Fairies, unicorns, dragons who breathe fire,
Anything you could possibly desire.
Fearsome pirates, sailing towards shore,
Nothing you could possibly ignore.
Rubies, emeralds, diamonds that gleam,
Who knows, maybe one contains your dream!

**Ivy Parker (10)**
Cheddar Grove Primary School, Bedminster Down

# Candy Land Nightmare

Oh no, pink terrifying mist and strange nightmares all over the place. A deep dark forest led me to a mysterious vortex. Moonbeams pulling me along in a candy rainbow full of mystery. An eerie fox came by my side with his tail in a box, he looked very cute though. I thought he was evil, but he was quite playful. I tried to stay calm but I was scared inside. Could he be my friend or was he a foe? Suddenly, the school bell rang. It was all a dream. I went to go outside, but all of a sudden, I saw a fox running along with his tail in a box. Was it a dream? No one knows for sure.

**Remi Davidson (8)**
Cheddar Grove Primary School, Bedminster Down

# Once Upon Luna's Dream

Once, there was this girl called Luna, and she would have bad nightmares, but one night, she had a good dream about birds flying over the sky while the sun was setting.

They brought her up to the sky, but Luna wanted to go down, but she couldn't go down because the birds could not glide down, so they dropped her on a trampoline. Luna said, "This is not my house." So she climbed up on the wall and wobbled along. She fell into another garden.

She sneaked into a house to see if it was hers. She shouted, "Yes! Yes! I've found my house."

**Millie Downs (9)**
Cheddar Grove Primary School, Bedminster Down

# Dream Dancer

I am a dancer,
Big and strong,
Never give up, all along.

I point my toes, flex them too,
Training every day is what I am trained to do.

Hip-hop, jazz, and lyrical too,
You may even see me flying in cheer too,

  **D** edicated,
  **A** thletic,
  **N** eat,
  **C** reative,
  **E** ntertaining.

My hair is always slick, to stop me from missing a trick,
I don't miss a beat, even if I am sick,
Because training every day is what I am trained to do.

**Maizie-Mai Clark (9)**
Cheddar Grove Primary School, Bedminster Down

# Dreams At Nan's

In my dreams every night I go to my favourite place,
Nanny's house is where it's at, a very magical space,
As I enter the dog barks and gives me fright,
Ah, I stroke his fur from day to night,
It is time to sleep real tight,
A dream inside a dream, what a strange place to be,
I'm at my other nanny's going on walks and climbing lots of trees,
I look for plants, birds and bees,
We learn a lot of things,
My nanny's place is where it's at,
It's the place I like to be.

**Tommy Hubbard (7)**
Cheddar Grove Primary School, Bedminster Down

# The Secrets Of The School!

Every night snuggled in bed,
Millions of dreams come into my head,
One adventure, one frightening,
Some nights I can have lightning,
A small figure passes the moon,
As she goes past with a zoom,
Nobody knows who she is,
Only because she goes past with a whizz.
A secret which has never been told,
But this tale is very old,
I turn around and close my eyes,
While the moonlight sky goes by,
Now I see a moonlit beam,
I woke up, and it was all a dream.

**Iola Jones (9)**
Cheddar Grove Primary School, Bedminster Down

# Dragon Dreams!

**D** uring the midnight,
**R** ight at twelve o'clock,
**A** lice, my magical dragon,
**G** lides down from Dragon Land,
**O** n my lap, she lies,
**N** ight is a magical time.

**D** arting to my house are my friends,
**R** ight at that moment, their dragons glide,
**E** agerly waiting to ride our dragons,
**A** t that moment we rise onto our dragons,
**M** ighty magic flies us high,
**S** pecial times are at midnight.

**Iris Hobbs (9)**
Cheddar Grove Primary School, Bedminster Down

# Monster Teacher

When I go to school,
My teacher is in a pool
Of slime drinking wine.

At playtime, the apparatus came alive
Shaking people off like flies

In the corridor,
The cleaning lady was mopping the floor,
Right next to the headmaster's door.

The headmaster's door was oozing with slime,
Oh gosh, it's the monster Oodaloer with tentacles left and right,
He really was a fright,
And I ran as fast as I could,
Out to the wood.

**Paisley Bishop (8)**
Cheddar Grove Primary School, Bedminster Down

# It's My Time To Shine!

One day in my dream,
I was something different, read and you'll see,
At school, it was a normal day,
Until the rain drained it away,
I was sad for a while until break time made me smile,
It was 'mugger' day!
Everyone was excited to play,
A match, a derby,
As we were playing I kicked the ball,
Surely it wouldn't hit the goal,
It went in,
And I celebrated with a grin,
I said, "It's my time to shine."

**Sennen Brown (10)**
Cheddar Grove Primary School, Bedminster Down

# Scary Fish

**S** houting loud noises upon the sea
**C** arefully looking under the deep, dark waters where fish will be
**A** cross a cave, a shark occurred
**R** ound the sea, my eyes got blurred
**Y** elling for help I drown in scary thoughts

**F** urther and further, darker and darker
**I** got lower and lower to get no oxygen
**S** taring down I fell to the bottom
**H** aving my last heartbeat before it ends!

**Eleanor Smith (8)**
Cheddar Grove Primary School, Bedminster Down

# Kittens

**K** ittens playing, kittens laughing, kittens everywhere
**I** ncredible kittens doing activities, phenomenal kittens eating food
**T** housands of kittens, all asleep, squashed in bed
**T** raining on a pitch for the big game
**E** xtraordinary kittens in a restaurant, serving people dinner
**N** ice kittens snuggling friends, all asleep on their lap
**S** trange colours on their fur: grey, black, brown and ginger.

**Calvin Rees (8)**
Cheddar Grove Primary School, Bedminster Down

# Once Upon A Dream

In my dream,
I can see,
Flying cats,
It's only a dream,
Can it be?
Or is it me?
Maybe not, it's just me, a dream,
On a tropical beach,
I eat a peach,
Is it magical?
No, of course not, because it's only just a dream,
All I think are my dreams,
Are they real?
What do I believe?
Can't stop, won't stop,
Should I believe?
Maybe not, it's only just a dream.

**Maya Savioli (8)**
Cheddar Grove Primary School, Bedminster Down

# A Little Monster In My Dreams

In my dreams every night,
I dream of a creature taking flight,
On his magic boots, he comes to me,
With the same old result, yay and yippee!
With a smile on his face, he takes me to a ship,
That takes me on a trip,
To a place which he calls home,
Off we get and enter it,
The magical place is new each night,
Finally, he told me Galore his name,
Then Bert was his name,
Each night it was different.

**Esme Carnevale (9)**
Cheddar Grove Primary School, Bedminster Down

# Dream Foxes

Every night when I go to sleep,
Dream foxes dance and leap.

Their elegant colours shining bright,
Even in the dead of night.

But when the sun comes out to play,
The dream foxes scurry away.

I've tried everything to get them in the sun,
But I guess the darkness is just more fun.

So if you ever get sad or have a fright,
The dream foxes will meet you at night.

**Norah Kebby (9)**
Cheddar Grove Primary School, Bedminster Down

# Royalty Loyalty

I live in a small house with a mouse,
I want to be royalty but I lack loyalty,
I'm in a palace that feels like glass,
With my friends, I lend my loyalty for some royalty,
I'm with my parents to bake, so I can have a piece of cake,
I have a flower, so I can take a shower,
I use a cookbook to look,
I had a crown and watched it drown,
I sold gold and I became very bold.

**Aisha Darboe (8)**
Cheddar Grove Primary School, Bedminster Down

# Dreamy Rats

Once, in my dream,
I saw fifteen rats.
I heard their leader,
Saying, "I love you."
They had bright colours,
And long snake-like tails.
I was horrified!

The next night,
I dreamed about,
Dreamy rats.
I loved them,
But I realised,
I had a nightmare yesterday,
And now today,
I'm not having a nightmare,
It was strange.

**Bobbie Earrey (9)**
Cheddar Grove Primary School, Bedminster Down

# Paradise

The paradise I dream of is the best you'll ever see,
As your dreams come true, you'll realise others should come too.
As they arrive the popularity starts to thrive.
As you explore and explore you'll start to get bored
Of glancing at their immaculate landmarks.
If you ever want to meet me,
That's where I'll be.
But then I realise it was all just a dream!

**Louis Morris (9)**
Cheddar Grove Primary School, Bedminster Down

# Gymnastics

I'm in a gymnastics studio
In my dream, I'm on the beam

In my dream, I am on the floor.

I can see my friend on the bars, doing a front flip off the bar
Crowds cheering for Gracie to win a medal.

**D** ogs flying
**R** ats eating
**E** lephant stomping
**A** nt hopping
**M** ouse crawling
**S** nake slithering.

**Gracie L (8)**
Cheddar Grove Primary School, Bedminster Down

# Animals

**A** s I close my eyes in the dead of night,
**N** odding off to dreams of a zoo, what a sight!
**I** n the cage, I get to go, because I am famous.
**M** any people form a line to stare at us,
**A** ll are amazed to see me with a Jesus lizard,
**L** ooking at him walk on water, what a wizard!
**S** un is up, so I'm sad that my fun dream is over.

**Charlie Pinder (8)**
Cheddar Grove Primary School, Bedminster Down

# Wolves Aren't Always Bad

A girl walks into the forest,
All alone, she is so honest,
A wolf jumps out from behind the bushes,
The girl's ruby eyes stare into the wolf, as her mind rushes,
Her bones are still,
The wolf transforms into a woman that
Kills the silence, and whispers, "Are you okay?"
The little girl runs into a tree, and nothing is heard.

**Lilly Hubbard (10)**
Cheddar Grove Primary School, Bedminster Down

# Once Upon A Dream

In my dreams, I meet Luke Littler
In my dreams, I meet the Bristol City players
In my dreams, I am a darts player
In my dreams, I want to meet all of the Bristol City players
In my dreams, I want to be a footballer
In my dreams, I want to win the Champions League, Premier League, FA Cup, the World Cup, Carabao Cup and the Player World Cup.

**Luca Britton (7)**
Cheddar Grove Primary School, Bedminster Down

# The Spider Shadow!

Spiders in my bed or are they in my head?
Are spiders green and why are they so mean?
Some are hairy, some can jump,
Some stare for hours planning to hunt.

Spiders live to make webs,
Sometimes they stick to my head.
With eight legs and fangs, a silk web in sight,
My fear is real, will I sleep tonight?

**Isla Brodribb (8)**
Cheddar Grove Primary School, Bedminster Down

# The Lost Horse

In my dreams at night,
My horse wanted to take flight.
I looked to my right,
What a beautiful sight.

I looked to my left and my horse had gone.
I thought this was wrong.
I found her trapped on a farm.
My dog ran up and jumped over the sty,
And released my horse into the evening sky.

**Emily Luke (9)**
Cheddar Grove Primary School, Bedminster Down

# Calvin-Robot

**C** alvin-Robot
**A** lways laughing
**L** oud voice
**V** ery talented
**I** ncredibly smart
**N** ever rude to others

**R** unning fast
**O** ne of a kind
**B** est friends with me
**O** utstanding personality
**T** housands of funny things.

**Neave Young (8)**
Cheddar Grove Primary School, Bedminster Down

# The Land Of Magical Dreams

**D** reams are full of adventures and fun,
**R** ed and blue confetti and more amazing colours,
**E** very dream is a different one,
**A** s crazy as you want,
**M** agical wherever you go,
**S** ome are happy and joyful, some are scary, some are sad, but every dream is different.

**Isla Green (10)**
Cheddar Grove Primary School, Bedminster Down

# The Fungus Land

In my dreams, I crash on an unknown planet
In my dreams, I see fungus everywhere
I smell rotten mushrooms
I see fungus monsters crawling around
Watch out! The fungus human will get you!
It will bite you with its razor-sharp teeth
Run, run, run, the fungus monster is here.

**Harry Cove (8)**
Cheddar Grove Primary School, Bedminster Down

# Football

In my dream, I wish to be a footballer,
Just like van Dijk.
In my dream, I dream of mega footballers,
Like Haaland, running across the pitch as fast as Messi,
as strong as Ronaldo.
I score a goal, the crowd yells, "Barney!"
Confetti falls down, like I dreamed of.

**Barney Downs (8)**
Cheddar Grove Primary School, Bedminster Down

# Aliens

Aliens up high,
In the sky,
Flying around the planets.

Swish, slam,
Wallop, bang,
The rockets take to the skies.

Flashing lights,
Swoops of colour,
Shooting stars above.

I wish my dreams could be like this forever.

**Florence Magor (10)**
Cheddar Grove Primary School, Bedminster Down

# Candy Land

Sparkles and shimmers ever so bright,
A sparkly creature dazzling in the light.
A delicious-looking treehouse in the moonlight.
It is a candy land in magical light,
Bright as the sun is the sunlight.
Cotton candy is as soft as a pillow at night.

**Ellie Payne (8)**
Cheddar Grove Primary School, Bedminster Down

# Cute Dogs

Cuddly dogs in my dreams,
Having a bath with me.
Young dogs having fun,
In a wet bun.
Dogs drying in the sky
Next to Dubai.
Never crying in the sky,
Whilst getting dry.
Kind dogs chasing cats,
Through the city and back.

**Woods Lott (8)**
Cheddar Grove Primary School, Bedminster Down

# Mythical Creatures

At night a girl slept,
In her comfy bed,
When a dragon knocked on her window,
She was afraid,
But she went,
She came to the forest,
With animals,
Mythical creatures,
They met up,
And had a party.

**Niamh Sheehan (8)**
Cheddar Grove Primary School, Bedminster Down

# Care About Nature

In my dreams every night
A bright green forest with lots of animals
I am with my cat, Buddy
Under the shade of a jade tree
I explore the extreme mountain
Suddenly, I become a nature expert.

**Oscar Taylor (8)**
Cheddar Grove Primary School, Bedminster Down

# Dog

**P** uppies flying in the sky
**U** p in the sky
**P** laying fetch in the sky
**P** opping
**I** ncredible dogs
**E** xtraordinary
**S** uper dogs.

**Jacob (8)**
Cheddar Grove Primary School, Bedminster Down

# Dreams

**D** reaming dinos
**R** eading rhinos
**E** ating elephants
**A** mazing gentlemen
**M** agic fairies
**S** tunning models.

**Alice-Rose Owen (8)**
Cheddar Grove Primary School, Bedminster Down

# My Best Dreams

Me and my friend at the city ground
Found Ronaldo's football boots and a football
I kicked the ball as high as light.

**Rocco Clark (7)**
Cheddar Grove Primary School, Bedminster Down

# My Family

My life is pretty amazing,
Like the stars at night that are blazing,
One thing that's important to me is my family.
Let me introduce you to my family,
Grandpa, who is affectionate while my heart starts to race,
Grandma, who is compassionate and my best mate,
My dad is smart and cheerful every day,
If something goes wrong, he saves the day.
My mum is smart and sweet, after all she's my heartbeat,
My two sisters are playful and always joyful,
Last but not least, my brother,
Who is sweet and cute and handsome too.
Well, that's my loving family,
Always adoring me while I feel grateful,
But also my beautiful family loves me too,
While we have fun, out in the sun,
With everyone.

**Ikham Chand (10)**
Durdan's Park Primary School, Southall

# An Astounding Adventure

*The Peculiar Letter*
As I drowse off into my soundly slumber,
My friend, Esme, encounters my cumber,
Her eyes like adamants,
Her expression with bafflement.
With the scent of lavender enwreathing her surroundings,
She bestows a piece of parchment which I assume nothing,
Yet the look on her face tells me otherwise.
Puzzled, I grab it, thinking of a prize,
But words that dance on the paper,
Look like a stranger.

*Mr Gerardo Patrive*
'Dear children,
Please listen!
My post in agony,
I beseech for company.
May you accommodate my dismal plea,
Or shall you cast aside me with glee?
It would be my utmost joy at the most,
If you advance your way to the forest with my post,

Where at last we shall arrive,
From Gerardo Patrive.'

*Esme's Sagacious Decision*
I avow with scepticism in my voice,
"It seems as if he were hoise!"
I believe it would be better to discover,
However, Esme aspires not to uncover.
Pointedly, I tell her that she will be disrepute,
Which leads to an exceedingly useless dispute.
While the letter - writhing and struggling to get free - is clutched,
My companion gives me an overall judge.
Reapproachful in my supportive suggestion,
She consents with an apprehensive smile unquestioned.

*The Battle*
With the exotic aroma enhancing the forest's elegance,
Its nature-filled beauty gives more than a glance.
The time-honoured, treasured trees bestride over ourselves with fatigue;
Flamboyant birds enchanting the lumid sky with physique.

Amiably, antique relics - like books and parchment - drift with ease,
And my uncertainty inaugurates to cease.
In the company of inquisitive vigilance, I seek,
For I can't enable trustworthy of the meek,
As me and Esme voyage through the woodlands with observant eyes,
My imagination debates whether my decision was wise.
*Crack!* I shift as fast as a flash of lightning,
Only to discover an Esme apologising.
Unruffled from my contemplation,
I ponder deeply which leaves no explanation.
However, I perceive of a shriek that terrorises my soul,
As I turn to find one of the most rambunctious, resentful roles:
The Shadow.
Attempting to get to the meadow,
We try to evade his cold-blooded clutch,
With as many charms flitting from our wands that we can budge.
Promptly, Esme forsakes me within a second,
Although I endeavour to inveigle her to bide as I beckoned.
The shadow, pursuing towards me with speed,
Forces me to strive and perpetually keep heed.

Despite my trepidation, I take a breath of mettle,
And I close my eyes like I was little.
*Boom!* I awake instantly as I hear,
A voice approaching me, calling out a, "Here!"
While I glance hastily at the peculiar monstrosity,
Out of the corner of my eye, I notice something that awakens my curiosity...

*The Troublesome Truth*
Under the canopy of trees that begin a frolic, the absolutely abnormal atmosphere appears to freeze,
With us approaching cautiously towards the ravenous beast as time is suddenly grasped and seized.
The shadow, unexpectedly tranquil, was keeping its obedience;
I was surprised by its most unusual peaceful patience.
Valiantly, I question why it was tempted to bring a fight -
It looked at me as if it'd never seen such a sight.
Monotonously, he told us in an eerie tone,
"I shall recite with the most detail I can muster that has been known,"
"Proceeding from region to region, I plead,
Which you comprehend, for a delightful, delicate deed,
As I laze there, unknowingly, dumbfounded,
Before I could get confounded,

I awake to find I'm taken into custody-"
However, before he could commence his tale to anybody,
I initiate to arouse from my rather flabbergasting doze,
As I unfurl my eyes which nobody knows.

*A Reminiscent Face*
Jolting with a start, I warily glance around,
Before I strand the comfort of my bed and steer towards the window without a sound.
The street lamp, which was luminous, grins broadly,
Yet a dark shape turns and winks at me before leaving shortly...

## Aishwarya Elanchellyan (10)
Durdan's Park Primary School, Southall

# My Lovely Friends

My friends are very nice,
Sometimes they call me mice,
When I go to school,
We are always cool,
And when it is Tuesday, I definitely go to school,
My friends said, "Do you have goggles for the pool?"
When I go home,
I never go alone,
When we go to each other's house,
We play a lot,
When I get there I knock,
My friend gets a shock,
We bash with each other,
My friend has a little brother,
We play games of fun quests,
We always are the best,
It's sad we are miles away from each other,
But we will meet on a sunny day,
When hope comes and light will bring joy,
We will always be a friend,
It will never come to an end.

**Maham Usman (10)**
Durdan's Park Primary School, Southall

# I Love My Nation (India)

With the Himalayas in the north
India in the south
Arabian Sea in the west
Bay of Bengal in the east
I love my nation
With developed culture
And beautiful sculpture.

They have no rest
To do their best at work
I love my nation
They give us rice in ration
They dress in the latest fashion
They have many inventions
Which are about fiction.

I love my nation
With the numbers of hill station
Which are god's creation
It gives us perfection
And saves us from tension
This is India which is a place of happiness.

**Avnoor Kaur Sran (10)**
Durdan's Park Primary School, Southall

# About My Family

I am going to tell you all about my family.
So, let's start with my dad.
He is kind, and when I get something wrong, he always helps me.
Mum: she is really nice, and she helps me and takes care of me.
Grandma: she is so happy, and she's come to Earth to make a bond with me and everyone else.
She helps me.
Brother: my lovely, trustworthy brother keeps me safe and always helps me.
He is like a boy who is nice.
Me/Nimrat: I am really kind and I help everyone in my class and I am really happy.

Thank you for hearing my poem!

**Nimrat Chahal (10)**
Durdan's Park Primary School, Southall

# Flying To Hong Kong

Flying to Hong Kong, a journey begun,
Through skies painted gold by the setting sun,
Winged chariot, swift through the air,
Towards a city where dreams declare.

Across oceans vast, our vessel flies,
To where neon lights pierce the night skies,
A fusion of cultures, a tapestry grand,
In Hong Kong's embrace, we'll land.

From soaring heights to streets below,
Where ancient temples and modernity glow,
A skyline etched in my memory strong,
As our plane carries us where we belong.

**Zaroon Butt (10)**
Durdan's Park Primary School, Southall

# The Dreams I Get

Sometimes my dreams get out of hand,
I get lost in a different land,
In a place no one knows,
Where the people wear posh clothes,
I see fairies fluttering,
No goblins spluttering,
Butterflies having the time of their lives,
And bees having fun in their hives,
Without being said,
I had fun just lying in my bed,
But remember...
*Your dreams have no boundary!*

**Jennah Samhan Hussain (10)**
Durdan's Park Primary School, Southall

# Sisters

Sisters are a gift
*'No matter where we go*
*No matter what we do*
*You will always have me*
*And I will always have you'*
The love and bond we share
Can never be replaced
I love my sisters
Always and forever.

**Avneet Kaur**
Durdan's Park Primary School, Southall

# Delightful, Daring Dragons

Dragons are big, dragons are small,
Personally, which is the prettiest of them all?
Either Fire, Water, Earth or Air.
Would you face one, would you dare?
Let me tell you about Fire with his horrifying eyes,
He stares into your soul, trying his hardest to make you cry.
His scales are cherry-red and his breath smells of smoke,
Careful if you get close, try not to choke.
Water is next, she's as clear as a jewel,
Her smooth, glowy scales would camouflage in a pool,
Her wings on her back flutter gracefully like a butterfly.
And her water-like features glow like a firefly.
Earth is beautiful, she has flowers on her back
To be honest, she's the kindest of the pack.
Covered in plants, dirt, moss and flowers,
Earth is gorgeous and holds all the powers.
Last but not least is their dear friend Air,
He isn't really known because he is so rare.
Hides among the clouds and is as white as the snow,
His eyes are practically diamonds, no one knows…

**Sophie Barron (11)**
Grange Farm Primary School, Leeds

# School Life

Schooling in classes that we would never miss,
Each led by the dedicated teachers we all know so well,
Teaching us to paint, write and even spell.
With each day comes a new lesson, we learn so much,
From our knowledge and their human touch,
Like our parents, our teachers encourage us with
All we have got, maximising their effort within
Their teaching time slot.
When the time comes
Where everyone's wild playtime is of course at
The time, stamp your feet, clap your hands
Children from so many lands.
Jump for joy, jump for fun,
Jumping is great for everyone.
After that,
People sing their song for maths in their
Minds, try, try and try, the more I try
The more I cry.
I practise with my
Heart and soul,
Yet I am not able to achieve my goal.

The next stage of the game is the wish that everyone
Makes it for lunch
When people eat a bunch.
After lunch, you may play a game called
Tig, but some people get hit, but it is just a bit
Then, another lesson comes, so on
And so on until it is hometime.
A long day has come to an end
Shadows of a long day keep going.
Threatening to barge into the next day and the next
And so on.
Till they hurt all along.

**Yakout Abdullah (9)**
Grange Farm Primary School, Leeds

# The Girl Of Dreams And Dance

A girl called Olivia,
With no right leg,
Dreams of a dancer,
Inside her head.

Water she drinks,
But did she know,
The cool summer breeze,
Turns into snow!

A portal she sees,
A portal she needs,
A portal forming,
The strange pink glowing.

A small leap through,
Olivia does,
And a wizard she's peering at,
Through the snow.

The wizard asks, "Who goes there?"
And a small voice peeps, "Is this your lair?"
He bellows, "Yes, now why are you here?
I've really waited for my beer!"

"I hear you grant special wishes,
Now I'd love to dance!"
"Alright, it's just a skip and a prance."
With a magical hand,
Her wish came true,
And a tutu she wore,
A dark navy blue.

World famous she became,
After that night,
Some who compete,
Have quite a fright.
Now the girl we know,
Olivia is,
She travels near and far,
And that's just about it.

**Manroop Lall (10)**
Grange Farm Primary School, Leeds

# Age By Age By Age

Hello, hello, hello, I'm a really new child
I'll one day be old, oh!
Hello, hello, hello, I'm a really young child
I'll one day be old, oh!
Hello, hello, hello, I'm now a ten-year-old child
I'll one day be old, oh!
Hello, hello, hello, I'm now a fifteen-year-old child
I'll one day be old, oh!
Hello, hello, hello, I'm now a twenty-year-old *adult*
I'll one day be old, oh!
Great news, I am a footballer, pro,
I'll soon be old, oh!

Hello, hello, hello, I'm now
A twenty-five-year-old, I'll soon be old, oh!
Hello, hello, hello, I'm now a retired thirty-year-old
I'll one day be old. Oh!
Hello, hello, hello, I'm now a relaxed thirty-five-year-old
I'll soon be old, oh!
Hello, hello, hello, I'm now a forty-year-old,
I'll soon be old, oh!
Hello, hello, hello, I'm now old, oh...!

**Harley Abbott (9)**
Grange Farm Primary School, Leeds

# The Fossil

Squishing my toes down in the sandy beach of Scarborough
I was as happy as a pig eating from a trough, picking a special seashell for my auntie Barbara.
I was instead delighted with the fossil I came across. A dreadful feeling came over me,
When I heard a very loud ground-breaking roar, knowing I was far from home, I spun my head around in glee.
But instead of seeing my daddy,
I saw a great big dinosaur! The fossil had taken me back in time
To a land of magnificent creatures, up hills and mountains I had to climb.
Eventually coming face-to-face with a T-rex's feature, strange eyes blinked back at me.
Mr T-rex, as I affectionately called him, was all I could see
And he was as friendly as could be.
Placing the fossil down on a rock,
I was pleased to be back on the beach with my family, finding my baby brother's sock.

**Michaela Upton (9)**
Grange Farm Primary School, Leeds

# Nightly Terrors

**N** ever have I ever thought I'd land in this dream,
**I** had always slept peacefully, that was until the scream.
**G** lancing side to side, all I see is a man,
**H** ow on earth did he find my clan?
**T** hud! He moves, lurking around me creepily,
**L** ightly, my eyes were watching his every move sleepily.
**"Y** ou're a pretty specimen," the man said with glee,

**T** his situation made me want to flee.
**E** very time this occurred, I was awoken swiftly,
**R** ight when I did, the headache that came straight after wasn't nifty.
**R** emembering them was never an issue,
**O** h, the times I had whilst crying into a tissue.
**R** ight when they stopped, I thought it was done,
**S** till, I guess you can never get rid of the unfun...

**Bianca Nowak (11)**
Grange Farm Primary School, Leeds

# In My Dreams

When I went to sleep, I dreamed! I don't know if it was a dream, but there was a unicorn flying over my head. It asked me if it could do an adventure, I said yes. It let me call the name Dawn, she had a gown when we were gliding to find the rainbow.
"Oh, no! It's raining!" said the unicorn. But we kept going, and there was finally a rainbow. It took six weeks to get the gold on the rainbow. She did have a pretty horn. We tried to get it. It was impossible. There were people asking where we were going.
The princess said, "Oh! I am going to find the gold on the rainbow."
The people said, "You can't! You will never get to the rainbow." The unicorn and the princess were on the news.
The princess is now a queen and the unicorn is famous.

**Darcy Long (8)**
Grange Farm Primary School, Leeds

# Mythical Art Animals

Once upon a time, there was a girl and a dog and they were best friends. The girl's name was Betty and the dog's name was Billy. Betty and Billy were skipping to the park until they ran into a portal. They ran into it because it was so pretty. "Wow, look it is amazing!" the dog barked.
"Look at the trees, the trees are pink; the sky is green and the grass is blue. Now look at the animals, like dragon unicorns. OMG! That animal over there is a tiger, horse, unicorn, dragon, snake, cat, dog, monkey and owl mixed together. That animal is amazing, Billy. Let's play all afternoon, it will be fun."
They went home and told their mum and dad about their day. Then Betty and Billy went to bed and fell asleep.
Betty woke up and it had been a dream. "Billy, it was a dream."

**Ava-Mae Parchment (8)**
Grange Farm Primary School, Leeds

# The Never-Ending Forest

Playing hide-and-seek with my friends,
I soon wander into a woods with no end,
I go deeper and deeper, it's starting to get dark,
I squeeze between trees and duck under bark,
I soon start to wonder when it will end,
I still continue, but I'm starting to get scared,
I wonder and wonder, *should I turn back?*
I look behind and see nothing but black,
I freeze for a second, I hear a crack,
I say hello but nothing comes out,
I soon start to walk, run, then sprint,
After a while, I realise I am lost,
I let out a scream and then an, "Eek!"
I am surrounded by spiders and monsters with claws, I close my eyes then open them again,
I soon realise I am just in bed,
And it was just a dream that was in my head.

**Lacey Johnson (10)**
Grange Farm Primary School, Leeds

# When I Go To Bed

**D** o I lie here in my bed with things running in my head?
**R** ainbows speak to me, but I can't hear what they have said
**E** veryone else is asleep in bed,
**A** mazing day beyond ahead, but there is something hiding in my shed
**M** agically, there is a unicorn longing to be fed

**N** othing is as scary as this
**I** am shocked at what this is
**G** remlins all over the place
**H** ow did they get here? They were smashing my plates
**T** oo scary to be true
**M** y cousin got me some plates that are new
**A** n exhausting day, need a good night's sleep, phew
**R** eady to go on a hike with my cousin, Jack
**E** veryone hide, the Gremlins are back.

**Kacie Pedder (9)**
Grange Farm Primary School, Leeds

# Dream Come True

On Christmas Eve, a young six-year-old girl called April was preparing to go to sleep.
She hoped she would wake up and have a nice, sweet treat.
Once she rested her eyes, she imagined and imagined.
Presents! Sweets! Love and joy. Oh, how much did she wish that would've happened.
Goodies, family or a roast chicken dinner
Like they all say, "Winner, winner, chicken dinner!"
April woke up, screaming at 6am
And kept on squealing, "Downstairs! Downstairs!" again and again
When she went down, it was all silent but ever so bright
All she dreamed of last night!
What an amazing sight!
There, above the door was a bunch of mistletoe
Some love may come shining, but I guess you will never know.

**Millie Hawes (11)**
Grange Farm Primary School, Leeds

# My Dream School

I dream of a school,
Not a normal one, one that's cool,
Full of breaks, full of fun,
And games when your art is done,
No oily dinners,
No unfair winners,
No speeding fines,
And definitely no boring times.

I dream of a school,
Not a normal one, one that's cool,
With gummy pencils,
Followed by chocolate stencils,
And Fidget pens,
Used in dens,

I dream of a school
Not a normal one, one that's cool,
Less history,
More geography,
Easier DT and harder ICT.

I dream of a school,
Not a normal one, one that's cool,
My teacher would be as friendly as a whale,
Who would give children free toys from the sale.

**Ameya Mishra (9)**
Grange Farm Primary School, Leeds

# Unicorn Land

In my dream, me and my friends were playing in the garden. As we were having fun, suddenly, we got teleported to a magical world in the middle of Saturn. We were wondering where we were when a unicorn suddenly appeared. The unicorn was rainbow coloured with a pink horn, a blue tail and sparkles everywhere. The unicorn took us to a pink castle with unicorn, horse, pony and Pegasus statues that sparkled in the night. As we walked inside, we saw fairies dancing. They said, "This place is the best place in the universe and you should stay here forever."

Then, suddenly, we were transported back. I felt happy when I went to this universe, but my mum woke me up for breakfast as it was nearly time for school.

**Mia Johnson (9)**
Grange Farm Primary School, Leeds

# Great Days And Bad Days

Mondays are good days, also fun days,
Tuesdays may feel like doomsday, but at the end, it's a cool day,
Wednesdays are my bad day, I'm tired at school,
But tomorrow is a great day,
Because our class visits the swimming pool.
Thursdays are great days, I go to swim in the pool, it's really cool,
Fridays are bad days, I say goodbye to my friends,
This is because the school week ends.
Saturdays I wake up, there's no school,
What shall I do with my day? Oh yes! I can go out and play tomorrow,
Sunday marks the end of the week. I'm back to school.
I've had great days and bad days, that's pretty cool.

**Leo Tempest (9)**
Grange Farm Primary School, Leeds

# Dreams

When eyes begin to close,
And people begin to doze,
When the sun fades away
And animals go to lie in their hay

A mysterious figure lurks through the shadows,
Waiting for a child who is drowning in sorrows
And just to make them worse
He casts upon a terrible curse.

For that night, when they go to sleep,
Things will seem incomplete
Pictures nailed to the floor,
And there aren't any doors.

You go downstairs to see your family,
Only to see this will end badly
You'll see them standing with a gun,
Then, you hear them all say, "Run."

**Miles Pierce (10)**
Grange Farm Primary School, Leeds

# A Mythical Land

One magnificent day I was going for an amazing stroll,
And I showed my great neighbour a magnificent show.
Then she laughed in joy,
Then I bought a toy.
Then I gave it to a boy,
Then he showed joy.
It was a great toy.
Then pirates captured me,
And raptured.
They took me to a terrifying dungeon that was as dark as the night sky.
Then they lied,
And said it. "Aye, aye."
You're pirates and "Ahoy ya matey."
Then a huge herd of unicorns saved me.
Thankfully then my fairies greeted me at the palace.

**Ellie Shirt (9)**
Grange Farm Primary School, Leeds

# A Little Girl Getting Lost

A little girl got lost in a forest. She tried to call for help. This is where it all began.

A girl called Isabel was getting ready to go to bed. Her mum was kissing her goodnight when she asked her mum, "Mum?"

"Yes, sweetie?"

"If I have a nightmare, do I get to come to your bed?"

"No not today, okay?"

The little girl went to bed and dreamed of being in a forest with scary tigers, hungry llamacorns ready to pounce. She called for help, she screamed, "Help me, help me!"

**Evie Smith (10)**
Grange Farm Primary School, Leeds

# Defend Your Dreams

When I walk onto the football field,
I am a defensive shield,
When the opposition attacks I will never yield.

When my team attacks everything is so smooth,
We get into the groove and make the other team move.

When I take a shot it's too hot to handle,
My team is on fire, like a candle.

Football brings the world together like no other sport,
It brings hope and joy to people all over the world.

Football is mine and helps me shine.
Football is a dream.

**Yuvraj Singh (8)**
Grange Farm Primary School, Leeds

# Once Upon Maya's Dream

There were once two explorers called Maya (me) and Poppy (friend). One day, we went exploring and got lost in the forest. So, Poppy dug a hole and found dragon and dinosaur bones. I was so scared but amazed and proud of myself.

After a day of decisions, me and Poppy decided, "We should find our way back." So, we got up and went. *Would we survive or not?*

After days of finding our way back, we found our way back and went to the museum to give them in.

**Maya Kaur (10)**
Grange Farm Primary School, Leeds

# The World On The Other Side

Every night, I look up to the starry sky
The beautiful shooting stars that pass me by
As I lie there in my room
I see a blinding bloom
I gaze out of my window
To find a small, hollow door
Which stands there in the centre of the moor
I look at the door to see
The handle and the missing key
I carefully open it
To unravel the dreamy world bit by bit
The world beyond
That I have always been fond of.

**Clarinda Martins (11)**
Grange Farm Primary School, Leeds

# The Day We Got Lost In The Forest

Me and Lucy were thriving
The moment we were arriving

Walking away from our home
Felt like moving away from a stone

In through the gate
Felt like being late

Moments after
Felt like I was tougher

Lucy screamed,
"What is that in-between?"

In the trees
We had seen

A monster or two
Had been staring at us like in a zoo.

**Arya Hainsworth (10)**
Grange Farm Primary School, Leeds

# Seasides

**S** and was sitting between my toes,
**E** veryone was moaning about sea salt up the nose,
**A** s we sat there on the beach,
**S** eagulls above us started to screech,
**I** was playing with my ball in the blue sea,
**D** own came the waves crashing over me,
**E** veryone was eating, but we only had chips,
**S** omeone took my sister's and she flips.

**Nevaeh Wilson (9)**
Grange Farm Primary School, Leeds

# Nightmares

Every night I lie in bed, I nearly
Get a good dream
Tonight, I had a nightmare.
I saw climbing swords which could
Move on their own
And they came closer and closer
And nightmare pigs,
Look, three piggies.
Tonight, I woke up
As scared as a fox.
Yes, I did die in the nightmare
Like splattered cream.

**Oscar Hainsworth**
Grange Farm Primary School, Leeds

# The Yellow Kite

In my dreams every night,
I see yellow kites.
They fly so high in the bright blue sky,
I feel so happy, I could cry.
What a beautiful sight,
I see every night.
The birds twitter as they fly by,
I always wonder if they're saying hi.

**Lily Rowland-Abram (9)**
Grange Farm Primary School, Leeds

# Dancing Queen

Once, I had a dream, it was about a dancer and she danced and danced until she couldn't. She also went to the finals. I said to the dancer, "You are really good at dancing."
She said, "Thank you, I could teach you if you want?"
"Okay, that's so nice of you. I bet you could go and dance for the queen."
"You are so nice to say that."
I said, "If you do, can I come?"
She said, "Yes, of course you can, Bea."
"Thank you so, so much, you're so much nicer than my dance teacher, she's just so mean to me, she makes me do too much."
"Well, you have to perform too!"

**Beatrix Giles (8)**
Hesketh-With-Becconsall All Saints CE School, Hesketh Bank

# Once, I Had A Dream

Once, I had a dream I was chased by a creature, which I cannot say. It was as black as night and as fierce as the wind. Once, I had a dream I was a beautiful ballerina, twisting in the moonlight. So quiet and free, I dreamt and dreamt. Once, I had a dream I was soaring through the sea, with a mystical mermaid right in front of me. I saw coral and fish in the sea, all right in front of me. Once, I had a dream I was lying in bed, thinking about my dreams, going on in my head.

**Madison Callaghan (10)**
Hesketh-With-Becconsall All Saints CE School, Hesketh Bank

# The Powerball

I always wanted to have superpowers, but I never got any! Until I felt something inside of me. It was a superpower. Yes! I was suddenly transported to a battlefield. Someone needed me but then I felt nervous. What would happen? But I had to fight. I used my powers a lot when I was fighting and they really came in handy. I defeated a lot of people too. Suddenly, I couldn't feel anything and I realised it was just a dream, but a fun one.

**Ted Roberts (7)**
Hesketh-With-Becconsall All Saints CE School, Hesketh Bank

# The Tale Of Marble Cheese...

Once, I had a dream...
There were three animals
One an Arctic fox called Lucy
A mouse called Fred
A guinea pig called Tom
Lucy carried Fred
Fred carried Tom
Lucy saw two fantastic monsters
That's how Lucy could register there was marble cheese to Fred
The planet looked tasty
She was in the middle
They landed on the land
They fell to their home
Galaxy Bears.

**Chloe Rey (7)**
Hesketh-With-Becconsall All Saints CE School, Hesketh Bank

# Roblox

Once, I had a dream...
I was playing Roblox on my computer, suddenly an NPC grabbed me and pulled me into the game
When I woke up I saw that the sun was sturdy
The trees were sturdy, everything was sturdy even the grass was sturdy
Then the NPC disappeared into thin air
Then dancing and singing chicken nuggets invaded the game
I realised I could leave so I left

Once, I had a dream...

**Janos Kelemen (7)**
Hesketh-With-Becconsall All Saints CE School, Hesketh Bank

# Once, I Had A Dream...

Once, I had a dream... I was in a rocket flying to space and then I stopped on Planet Zoo. *Zoooom!* The rocket was still on, Tom turned it off. He looked up at the sky and saw something. A pig! Then a rat and a cat and a monkey!
Once, I had a dream... I was in space and saw animals flying up in space sky. The sky was dark and purple and there were loads of planets, colourful planets.
Once, I had a dream...

**Freya Sutton (8)**
Hesketh-With-Becconsall All Saints CE School, Hesketh Bank

# Can I Decide?

Once, I had a dream, what was it going to be?
A firefighter being famous and being yourself!
I saw a fireman digging a tunnel to the sea
And a famous pop star invited me to the sea for a concert
And last but not least, I saw me in the mirror
And I didn't want them again
I saw me.
Once, I had a dream about firemen, pop stars and me.
I wonder what I'll dream next!

**Harrison Costello (8)**
Hesketh-With-Becconsall All Saints CE School, Hesketh Bank

# The Big Magical Imagination

To play football on the moon with my friends and get a magic dog before the world ends
I will try to meet an alien before I am ill and fly and meet a bird who I think is a nerd
We will fly and go to cafes and meet a fox who is funnily named, Mof
And Mof said, "Hello little couple you really do cuddle; please don't give me a snuggle because they are a bit too tight."

**Immanuel Darby (8)**
Hesketh-With-Becconsall All Saints CE School, Hesketh Bank

# Once I Had A Dream...

S inging famously in front of fifty thousand people.
C uriously dreaming how many fans love me.
H appily enjoying singing when a fan throws a round red apple like a ball.
O wning a mansion, singing in the shower.
O wning a stadium, practising singing in front of my family.
L oving my fans and enjoying singing.

**Khloe Carter (8)**
Hesketh-With-Becconsall All Saints CE School, Hesketh Bank

# Flying

I fly so high in the sky seeing the trees and all the bees
I like to swim, I love to run but most of all I like to fly in the sky
I feel so free like a bee
So high in the sky, all the birds singing with me in the sky
I fly so fast in the sky
I love to fly like a plane in the sky
But when I wake from my amazing dream I feel so strong.

**Leo Manchester (10)**
Hesketh-With-Becconsall All Saints CE School, Hesketh Bank

# My Dream Of Fairies

Once, I crash-landed in a strange
World of glittering magic.

Then, two fairies arrived called
Fairy Leaders Freya and Rosie.
Freya was a flower fairy.
Rosie was an animal fairy.

When I saw them, I turned into a cat fairy.
Freya used her powers and
Rosie turned me into a cat fairy.
I had so much fun!

**Eloise Biggs (8)**
Hesketh-With-Becconsall All Saints CE School, Hesketh Bank

# Once Upon A Dream

Once, I had a dream about cute hamsters,
They talked to me,
I talked back,
I was the only person who could understand hamsters,
Some of the hamsters could write,
I took them to school on 'bring our pet to school day',
The hamsters jumped everywhere,
Everybody laughed.

**Phoebe Barrett (7)**
Hesketh-With-Becconsall All Saints CE School, Hesketh Bank

# What's Going On In My Dream?

Famous footballers, flying fairies, dancing wizards, royalty, pirates, superpowers, teachers, getting lost, builders, fighting, food, dragons, clowns, astronauts, unicorns, dinosaurs, writers, spiders, athletes, monsters. What's going on in my dream? Say, what's going on in my dream?

**Scarlett Bailey (9)**
Hesketh-With-Becconsall All Saints CE School, Hesketh Bank

# Once Upon Casey's Dream

Butterflies fly as high as the sky,
The green grass is beautiful and soft in a world of peace,
The animals came up to you,
To say hello,
While you're in the middle of nature,
And you can feel fantastic,
Dancing animals right in front of your face.

**Casey Ryan (8)**
Hesketh-With-Becconsall All Saints CE School, Hesketh Bank

# Best Day Ever

High in the sky,
Me and my family have dragons,
Roar, roar, roar,
We sit upon a hill,
I had long sat on,
Then we ate KFC whilst I played football,
It was so fun,
The KFC was delicious,
It was a good, fun day.

**Rosie Taylor (8)**
Hesketh-With-Becconsall All Saints CE School, Hesketh Bank

# The Magical Fairy And The Pony

Once upon a time, there lived a magical fairy. She went flying with her magical pony but, just then, she noticed there was something in the bush. It was a baby rabbit. She was very lonely, so she told the fairy and then she took the rabbit home.

**Isla Griffiths (10)**
Hesketh-With-Becconsall All Saints CE School, Hesketh Bank

# The Great Roar

Once, I had a dream... of very shiny stars so bright. I could barely see, it felt like I was in a magical world. I was dreaming of a lion roaring in the moonlight, as I rode all the way back home.
But this time it was true!

**Millie Costello (10)**
Hesketh-With-Becconsall All Saints CE School, Hesketh Bank

# Once Upon My Dream

Once, I had a dream.
I saw a fireman who went to the moon. A unicorn came with powers, a dragon that breathed fire out of its mouth and pop stars who had a band.
I also saw a cheese man.

**Jenson McDougall (7)**
Hesketh-With-Becconsall All Saints CE School, Hesketh Bank

# Extreme Imaginations

Once, I had a dream
I was swimming in whipped cream
My dog got a fright in the middle of the night
I was riding a llama while wearing my pyjamas

*Extreme!*

**Henry Tiltman (8)**
Hesketh-With-Becconsall All Saints CE School, Hesketh Bank

# Once Upon Libby's Dream

The world of nature,
The trees are up high,
The flowers are a colour,
Which is one of a kind,
The grass is so green and fresh,
The birds are singing in the trees.

**Libby Manchester (8)**
Hesketh-With-Becconsall All Saints CE School, Hesketh Bank

# Darth Of Death

The stars are so bright
When I look at Yoda, I see
Darth Vader looks at me
And sees Mace Windu
After the death of the Death Star began
Darth Maul appeared...

**William Latham (7)**
Hesketh-With-Becconsall All Saints CE School, Hesketh Bank

# Up In The Cold Starlit Night

Up in the cold starlit night,
Blossoms bloom with colours bright,
Unicorns fly high up in the sky,
Twirling and twisting higher and higher,
Passing me by,
Their manes are as hot as fire,
And their horns are as cold as ice,
But their skin is as soft as a cloud,
Candy canes and silver canes glow and shine,
As little dragons pass me by line by line,
Then out of the blue, butterflies as big as crystals wrap around me like a blanket,
Their wings are like rainbows,
And their heads are as small as cubes of ice,
All of a sudden, they prance around me holding hands,
They come and I join them too,
But then my cloud dives down,
Now I think the fun will end,
Just then I see houses holding treats,
And pink trees that can bend,
But for now,
Maybe, just maybe, I'll see them all again.

**Moriah Pietropinto (9)**
Kingsway Junior School, Watford

# The Endless Void

In the robot city
Where the night is day
The android leader
Comes out to play.

He's tall and tough
He's lean and mean
The android leader
Is a smart machine.

I'm here with Skelly
He's my pal
We're gonna escape this city…
Somehow.

The ground beneath us
Begins to shake
As the world around us
Starts to quake.

An endless void
Is what we see
This pit of darkness
Was bigger than me!

We fall into the void
With a thud and a bump
When three portals appear
Making us jump.

'Past', 'Future' and 'Present'
Is what I can see
"Pick a portal!" yells Skelly
So 'Past' it will be.

I get to the past
But this is not right
I see no friends here
Not one in sight.

It must be wrong
I have to go back
Maybe the 'Future'
Would keep me on track.

In the future
Is where I arrive
The only human here
That is even alive.

Surrounded by robots
In a city of tech
This future city
Looked like a wreck.

Please, oh please
May portal three
Be the one
To set us free.

Portal to the present
Let's try you
Hope and pray
Is all I can do.

Feeling scared
Is all I feel
Portal three
You'd better be real.

Falling fast
And spinning around
I suddenly...
Can't hear a sound.

I open my eyes
With shock and see
That I am in my bed...
I am free!

## Riley Wootton-Ward (8)
Kingsway Junior School, Watford

# My Time Control App

I've got an app that controls time,
I made it on my own, it's mine, all mine!
Check this out, I'll enter a race,
Even though last is always my place.
Let's slow things down, I'll walk and even sit down,
While all the others in sweat they drown,
Urgh, ads on TV, boring!
Let's speed things up before I start snoring,
They sound like chatty little chipmunks.
Time to stop the app,
It's as simple as *tap, tap, tap*,
Oh, now time's just stopped,
I try to pause it, but it won't unlock!
I'm travelling back, everything's shifting in size,
I'm in an era I don't recognise!
I think my app has some minor flaws,
Because now I need to avoid being eaten by dinosaurs!

**Mia Koster (10)**
Kingsway Junior School, Watford

# Dancing Under The Moonlight

Under the moon so bright and clear,
We dance and twirl without a fear
In the night's embrace, we take delight
Dancing under the stars shining so bright
With giggles and laughter, we dance around
Our feet tapping to a joyful sound
We sway and spin like fireflies in flight
In this magical dance, oh, what a sight
The moon's beam guides us with its gentle glow
As we dance and prance, putting on a show
With each leap and twinkle, we feel so free
Dancing under the moon, just you and me
So, come little ones, let's dance and play
Under the moonlight let's light up the way
With smiles on our faces, we'll dance with glee
In this moonlit dance filled with pure jubilee.

**Sherrie-Ann Gorman (8)**
Kingsway Junior School, Watford

# The Pirate Adventure

Deep in the sky, a pirate ship awaits an adventure, waiting for you to read...

Captain Jack rambled, "Sea monster! North!"
The others urgently tightened the ropes and Captain stared
But an unloyal pirate shouted.
A sea serpent said, "You were unloyal to my family and lied,
So you shall be imprisoned in the sky."

And that pirate was named Apollo
But he was just left solo.

Seconds later, the ship was sinking
And at the time, Captain was drinking.

So, he choked and that night then led to his fate.
He asked the pirates to guard the gate.

But no one was there, then there was one pirate called Percy
Who was given mercy.

**Elva Tse (7)**
Kingsway Junior School, Watford

# Cavemen

What did cavemen wear on their feet?
Cobblestone or gems, from the Isle of Crete.
What did cavemen use for doors?
Giant boulders, did they even have floors?
What did cavemen even eat?
Vegetables, or maybe meat?
What did cavemen even wear?
Clothes that were made out of hair.
How did cavemen get their food?
They'd hunt for fish if they were in the mood.
What did cavemen have as pets?
Animals that were not a threat.
Could cavemen sit on stools?
No, because they didn't go to school.
What could cavemen even play on?
Not bouncy balls and not even a crayon.

**Leo Gladdy (9)**
Kingsway Junior School, Watford

# Angry Dragon

In front of your eyes, an angry dragon lay,
Still had not been slayed.

To go inside the deep, dark cave,
You, my friend, must be brave.

Inside lurks a creature grim,
I know you'll be scared of him!

Skin very rough,
Which makes him tough.

If the dragons near,
It will smell your fear.

In some way, we must reveal,
We are dragons! *We are real!*

**Vyan Shah (10)**
Kingsway Junior School, Watford

# My Nightmare

So, I was playing football. Then, a spaceship sucked me up and sent me to the forest. I ran, trying to leave. I saw where it ended. But when I left, it just teleported me back! I ran so much that I got tired. When I got up, I ran west and I saw a house with people shouting, calling, "Help me!" I ran to the house and there, I saw the Grim Reaper stabbing my friend. Then I woke up, just to realise it was all just a nightmare.

**Lorenzo Righi (9)**
Kingsway Junior School, Watford

# Abyss

My head hit the bed as I fell into the abyss,

I thought it was a joke,
Until I realised I was surrounded by smoke,

**A** figure with a grin,
**B** y the time it popped out the rim,
**Y** our inner self screamed,
**S** uddenly it went blank,
**S** uch I wanted a friend,

I wanted this dread to end,
And then I sat in my bed.

**Fatema Ali (11)**
Kingsway Junior School, Watford

# Monkeys In Town Today

We are monkeys, and we're here to stay,
We are the baddest in this town today,
I could hear them roar,
From the forest next door,
I heard one of them explain,
"Let's get the train!"
"Let's go into town and dress as a clown!"
I called my mum, "Let's have some fun!"

**Cara Perkins (8)**
Kingsway Junior School, Watford

# The Birds

Birds are sweet and all birds tweet
Pigeons fly while the flowers bloom
But be careful 'cause all birds go *zoom!*
Hummingbirds singing all around town
Cockatoos flying up so high
Crows are crazy
But other birds are calm
Who cares though? All birds are cute.

**Alyssa Kimpton (8)**
Kingsway Junior School, Watford

# Dragon Wagon

There once was a dragon,
Who got stuck in a wagon,
He waggled his tail,
To draw attention to the whale,
Soon he was free to eat his dragon Magnum,
He ran and hid,
That's what he did,
So, we waved goodbye,
When he was far and high.

**Madison Corcoran (8)**
Kingsway Junior School, Watford

# Once Upon A Dream

Once, I had a dream, that I could be a girl in a world of fantasy.
Once, I had a dream, where I was floating in the air, like a little beam.
Once, I had a dream, I was filled with glee, dancing with happiness in a field of green.
Once, I had a dream, of us all, because poem or tome, novel or book, just take a look and you will see your own fantasy.

My dreams,

**D** reams are what I see every night, when I sleep,
**R** eaching forward to a potential of glee,
**E** very night, when I fall asleep, gnomes and goblins,
**A** nd fairies come to visit me and they won't leave because it's my fantasy,
**M** y dreams come to an end and I have to say goodbye to my friends.

**Sanaya Sookhun (9)**
Merton Junior School, Basingstoke

# Cloudy Dream

Once upon a dream, I woke up to a gleam
The stars' light brought all my might
I look to my right and see a sight to behold
It's night's edge doing a pledge
I am part of the cloud.

Once upon a dream, I woke up to a gleam
The stars' light brought all my might
I look to my left lifting my head
It's a superior angel with an interior
I am part of the cloud

I am the cloud.

**Daniel Winczewski (9)**
Merton Junior School, Basingstoke

# Demon And Dreams

*Demon*
Lurking in the darkness, out of sight
Lies a creature that is evil and ghastly
Here in this wet, putrid cave lies a demon
A demon that cackles and performs bloody sacrifices
And deadly magic.

*Dreams*
"What are dreams?" asked the boy,
"Why, dreams are when you lie down and relax," said I
When I asked four educated boys what a dream was...

**Sivani Vattikuti (9)**
Merton Junior School, Basingstoke

# Dream

I woke up from my bed
I looked at my jars
Where my coins were
I saw something that I'd seen before
It all flew out of the jars
It went for a ride
But before I went back to bed
I heard a clatter somewhere
It shot to the sky
Making a firework
Then I went back to bed
After what I saw.

**Phoebe Pearce (8)**
Merton Junior School, Basingstoke

# Summer

Summer is a time to have fun and enjoy the sun,
The days are long and warm,
But are also filled with energy and laughter,
I can smell the warm, inviting breeze,
Welcoming me into its open arms,
A cool treat, melting away in the summer heat,
Summer is the time to create memories and enjoy the sun.

**Arzoo Ghale (9)**
Merton Junior School, Basingstoke

# Monsters

In my dreams tonight,
I see a green monster with great big bushy hair,
With fur so bright and claws so sharp,
Their tails are long and glow in the dark,
Their eyes are red as blood,
Their breath smells like fish.

**Emily Cox (9)**
Merton Junior School, Basingstoke

# My Hairdressing Poem

I wish I could be a hairdresser and go into an imaginary world.
Like sleeping outside in your dressing gown
and have a portal that I lean into and fall down
down, down, down, into a black hole that could go out of this world and into space.
I wish I could see a bright rainbow unicorn tonight
and wake up and see people begging for hair.
So this is what I'll do; I wish I could help people, be kind and generous like me
and people's dreams come to life with a click of my fingers
on the count of one, two, three. I ran,
help with whatever,
follow your friends and delight,
feel the need from people to find
her giving you food.
I can help you every day, me, Tilly-Rose, and help your hairstyle.
I travel straight to Spirit City Rainbow Chocolate
even covered in rainbow goo.
There are different hairystyles
please, oh please be careful with your hair.

Follow, rushing, reading, colourful,
Oh, this is for your hair.
You can choose out of these hairstyles
chocolate, marshmallow
there are so many different colours and flavours so delightful and helpful.

**Tilly Randall (10)**
Newton Longville CE Combined School, Milton Keynes

# The Archipelago Of Oddness

On a cold, stormy night, I fell asleep,
And woke up on an island full of sheep,
My eardrums were beating at the sound of the bleating,
As I discovered the harbour was wool,
My brain started to become full,
I ponder what is happening to me,
I'm teleported to an island that's 2D,
On this island, left and right are out of sight,
In the distance, I see some people and don't know what they're doing,
Turns out, a boss fight is brewing,
Just as I'm becoming entertained,
I'm teleported to Inverted Island, which is insane,
I walked on the sky, which wasn't actually high.
My dizziness was beyond comprehension,
Until my arrival on the Island of Depression,
As tears went by, I also started to cry,
Until finally, I awoke in my bed.

**Jack Dimmock (11)**
Newton Longville CE Combined School, Milton Keynes

# The White Room Of Life

A bee-like buzz repeats as a nostalgic film plays,
On the empty, white walls, it sends me into a haze.

It showed my mum holding me in a hospital bed,
People stared as my name was said,
It faded to another place in time,
To when I could speak,
In my old house on the main street.

Yet again, it faded to another memory,
However, this one definitely didn't give glee,
I was in the ocean, being tossed and hurled,
I wasn't in the blank, white world,
I thought I was going to drown,
I screamed and shouted, but there was no sound.

Startled, I suddenly jumped up,
Feeling as if I would throw up,
I was back in my bedroom, warm as toast,
But when I looked out the window, I was on the coast.

**Maisey Mullins (11)**
Newton Longville CE Combined School, Milton Keynes

# Around A Dreamworld

Suddenly, I'm out of my warm comfy bed,
Pincers pierce the ground as I enter this new world instead,
Eight legs dance as a web carefully unwinds,
I quicken my pace not daring to look behind,
Now I'm wishing I am in different places,
A house made of chocolate and strawberry laces,
I shut my eyes as I am transported,
It's exactly like a fairy tale story,
My eyes widen with delight and a grin spreads across my face,
I wonder who lives here, oh, it's such a wonderful, lovely place,
Now I'm back in my room with soft pillows,
No more delicious, squishy marshmallows,
What will tomorrow's dream bring?

**Ruby Dobson (11)**
Newton Longville CE Combined School, Milton Keynes

# When I Wish Upon A Star

I wish I was an athlete who ran hundreds of miles,
I wish I was a builder who fixed a lot of tiles,
I wish I was a swimmer who swam with great white sharks,
Or even just a person who played in a park.

I wish I was a baker who baked fresh bread,
I wish I was a doctor who fixed people's cracked heads,
I wish I was an actress stepping on stage,
Or even just a geologist examining jade.

I wish I was a police officer who stops lots of crimes,
I wish I was someone who only mimed,
I wish I was a dancer who danced the night away,
Or even just a girl who woke up in her soft comfy bed today.

**Elia Sepede (11)**
Newton Longville CE Combined School, Milton Keynes

# Oh, How I Wish

Oh, how I wish to be in a land full of sweets,
Oh, how I wish to have a floor of marshmallow beneath my feet.
Oh, how I wish to have trees with a sugary swirl,
Oh, how I wish to have a castle entrance with candy curls.
Oh, how I wish to have walls made of water paper,
Oh, how I wish everyone will come except my haters.
Oh, how I wish to have my own Haribo throne,
Oh, how I wish to have a bowl made of ice cream cones.
Oh, how I wish to keep my sweet tooth,
Oh, how I wish to grow up but never forget my youth.
Oh, now I wish to have an ice cream sundae,
Oh, how I wish every day could be a fun day.

**Harriet Hibbert (11)**
Newton Longville CE Combined School, Milton Keynes

# Slime

Suddenly, I find myself out of my warm comfy bed,
And in a distant mysterious world instead,
Everywhere I see is plastered in slime,
Making the walls very hard to climb.

Then I have the strangest urge,
To follow the man who has just emerged,
From the grimy bar,
And got inside his slimy spluttering car.

I shout, "Come back here!"
But the car is not coming near.
I dash off in chase,
But, all of a sudden, the slime has a face.

It's engulfing me like I'm drowning in a pool,
Then my mum shouts, "Get up, you'll be late for school!"

**Freddie Everitt (11)**
Newton Longville CE Combined School, Milton Keynes

# The House Of Wonders

The resplendent House of Wonders,
Peaceful like a dove,
Really makes you ponder,
On what there is to love.
You open the door,
It creaks with the floor,
Now the smile you once wore,
Is now but a thought.
Rats crawl up the walls,
Ants march out of the hole,
As darkness brings sadness,
Into this world, which drives you to madness.
You walk to the door,
But you cannot escape,
You fall to the floor,
And accept your new fate.
You hear something weird,
And then you are led,
Without any fear,
Into your mysterious, wonder bed.

**Finlay Doyle (11)**
Newton Longville CE Combined School, Milton Keynes

# My Passion For Fashion

I dream of strutting down a scarlet-red carpet,
Thousands of people shouting my name.
The thought of spotlights shining on me,
The crowd would go wild and cheer when they see.

Me, a fashion model?
Standing on stage?
Oh, it would be such a wonderful thing!
Judges would judge my fabulous style,
And camera lights would flash as photos are taken.

I would be famous and in magazines,
Posing for pictures and taking autographs.

Next thing I know,
I'm back in my warm, comfy bed.
Wondering if my magical dream will ever come true.

**Lillian Irving (10)**
Newton Longville CE Combined School, Milton Keynes

# The Solemn Soldier

I had a dream that wasn't so good,
About me and a child who just watched and stood.
There we were on a deserted harbour,
Watching a soldier who was once a barber.

Now he's left for the war,
The last time we saw him was on the shore,
Gloomy clouds hung over us,
As furious waves crashed against the rocks. *Crash!*

We knew this wasn't going to end well,
But I wasn't brave enough to come out of my shell,
That was the first I'd ever seen of him,
And also the last.

The next thing I know, I'm in my cosy, warm bed.
I've woken up, something's thudding in my head.

**Elia Piacquadio (11)**
Newton Longville CE Combined School, Milton Keynes

# Once Upon Milly's Dream

I long to be brave,
To be okay with change.
I wish to be kind,
And look after my mind.

To let go of a loss,
And always be my boss.
To be the best friend,
And know that they'll bend.

Like Dr King who stood up for his race,
To never care about my face.
To build the right crew,
But not bite off more than I can chew.

I wish to always try,
But if I lie,
I shall never achieve,
I'll try to believe.

**Milly Alderson (11)**
Newton Longville CE Combined School, Milton Keynes

# Oh, How I Wish

Oh, how I wish I was an actress starring in a film.
Oh, how I wish my film went viral all around our realm.
Oh, how I wish I was stepping up on stage holding an Oscar.
While then, I just used to be a girl going to Costa.
I used to have no money, none at all.
While now, I'm a billionaire holding fancy balls.
Now I stay up late dancing the night away.
But that was all a dream and I'm just a girl who woke up in her comfy bed today.

**Amelie Stephenson (10)**
Newton Longville CE Combined School, Milton Keynes

# Formula One

**F** ormula One: the height of racing.
**O** scar Piastri: leading the pack.
**R** ed Bull, struggling for pace.
**M** ax Verstappen is at the back.
**U** nderdogs continue to impress.
**L** awrence Stroll funds Aston Martin.
**A** ston Martin drives like rookies in Kartin.

**O** scar Piastri still leading the pack.
**N** ot giving up hope, keeping Max at the back.
**E** nding the race in first...

**Christian Rushton (11)**
Newton Longville CE Combined School, Milton Keynes

# My Dream To Change The World

I wish I could help the less fortunate,
And be grateful for what I have.
I hope to be looked up to,
An inspiration to do better.
I dream of all the changes I can make,
To this imperfect world.
I want to give hope to people around me,
That need it.
But then I found myself in my warm and cosy bed,
Hoping for my dreams to come true.

**Annabelle Terry (11)**
Newton Longville CE Combined School, Milton Keynes

# The Flying Express

Blitzing through the sky
Beginning to fly
The train is on its way
Flying fast every day
Passing by Big Ben
Over a field of hens
The train reaches its stop
And it lets you drop
Down, down, down
But don't you frown
Because before you know it
You've landed in Niagara Falls.

**Matthew Bebbington (11)**
Newton Longville CE Combined School, Milton Keynes

# Fame!

Once, I dreamt of being famous,
Cameras flashing and calling my name,
Signing autographs all day long,
This felt lonely and wrong,
I felt weary and no one could hear me,
Slowly, I woke up in despair,
Was that all a dream? Was I ever even there?

**Evie Bampton (10)**
Newton Longville CE Combined School, Milton Keynes

# The Ice Cream Crows

As I walked through a dimension of crows
Hundreds of ice creams are being thrown
I wake up from my dream
I see a crow on my window
As I look below, I see an ice cream cone
I'm not sure if I was hallucinating but I'm sure I saw it clone.

**Poppy Hack (10)**
Newton Longville CE Combined School, Milton Keynes

# If I Were An Artist

If I were an artist, I would become inspirational for kids.
If I were an artist, my paintings would be noticed by others.
If I were an artist, people would ask for my signature.
If I were an artist, this wouldn't be a dream.

**Emily Todd (11)**
Newton Longville CE Combined School, Milton Keynes

# My Castle Upon The Clouds

I like to drift off to my castle on a cloud where it's only happy thoughts and crying's not allowed.
I love to sit and play with all of my friends, we will run round for hours and the fun will never end.
In my castle on a cloud I feel happy and excited and when I see all the sweets I look delighted. In my castle on a cloud.

I love to run away to my castle on a cloud. Where we can sit in the grand living room and there is room for a crowd!
In my castle on a cloud there are grand chandeliers in every single room and outside the golden walls an orchestra playing a melodic tune.
As I sit on the ground I watch the vivacious fairies ahead turn round and round in my castle on a cloud.

As I relax upon a marshmallow cloud, I realise my time has ended for tonight but meet again I tell you we might.
I must tell you now to always believe, know that you must never deceive.
Know you have to do the right thing and know this wondrous time will ring again.
Not everything is like a big castle on a cloud but make the world yours and be proud!

**Lyra Henri (9)**
St Joseph's Catholic Primary School, Newbury

# The Last Minute

Welcome to the Santiago Bernabéu Stadium. Today you will see the most intense match ever. The teams are Cristiano Ronaldo, Lionel Messi, Kylian Mbappé, Erling Haaland, Taha and lastly Thibaut Courtois.
And the opposing team is Luis Suárez, Neymar Junior, Karim Benzema, Jude Bellingham, Robert Lewandowski and ter Stegen.
The match has started. Ronaldo passes to Messi. Messi passes to Ronaldo. Ronaldo shoots and the ball is in the back of the net. It is one zero. Suárez passes to Neymar. Neymar passes to Lewandowski. Lewandowski shoots and it's a goal. The referee blows the whistle for half-time.
Ronaldo dribbles, but it is a great tackle from Bellingham. Haaland with the kick. He passes to Ronaldo but Suárez slide tackles Ronaldo in the last minute of the game. Taha is taking the free-kick. He shoots and it's a goal.
Taha is celebrating with his teammates and lifting the Champions League trophy.

**Hujatullah Taha Maail (9)**
St Joseph's Catholic Primary School, Newbury

# Monsters Of The Dark

One night I was on a walk with my family
When a sudden wind blew over me
I turned around to see them gone
And got a shivering feeling something went wrong
I flew up into the air
But all I could see was the darkness out there
There were monsters hiding in the black
That's why I froze when something touched my back
I didn't want to turn around
Scared of what I may have found
I felt it creeping up on me
But what was it? I wanted to see
Did it have razor-sharp claws and millions of eyes?
Well, that would make a nasty surprise
Turning around to see what was there
And what it was it gave me a scare
To see my father standing there!

**Millie Pavey (10)**
St Joseph's Catholic Primary School, Newbury

# Strange Dreams

   **S** piderwebs everywhere,
   **T** he three friends walk to the frightful fair,
   **R** ain pouring on the head,
   **A** s germs are about to spread,
   **N** ext, we see a hand popping from the ground,
   **G** ood that
w **E** have turned around,

   **D** o this when you see a ghost,
   **R** un to the creepy-looking host,
   **E** at the grapes and you'll be safe,
   **A** s midnight falls you start to see a grave,
   **M** uch too late to talk or think,
   **S** o you start to feel like you are going to sink.

**Natalia Brydniak-Musal (9)**
St Joseph's Catholic Primary School, Newbury

# Candyland!

**C** andyland is a place to visit in your dream land.
**A** nd everything is made of candy in this land.
**N** o one can be sad in this magical land.
**D** ream each night, so you can visit this majestic land.
**Y** ou will enjoy yourself in the realm of Candyland.
**L** oving everyone is the main rule of the land
**A** ll people young and old are welcome to my special land.
**N** ot everyone has to like candy to enjoy Candyland
**D** reams are brought to life in Candyland.

**Sophie Sharma (9)**
St Joseph's Catholic Primary School, Newbury

# Dreams

**D** odging zombies and dodging anacondas now is the time to be brave,
**R** acing cars and racing people are way different, especially with cars,
**E** lections, elections, nothing better than winning elections,
**A** hoy, ahoy, maybe being kidnapped by pirates isn't the best thing,
**M** oments, moments, maybe we should appreciate before the momentum is gone!
**S** ilence, silence, maybe it should be the time to fall asleep with silence in our hands and time to have dreams.

**Eva Brites (9)**
St Joseph's Catholic Primary School, Newbury

# I Wonder

Dragons and dinosaurs dancing up high,
Loyal loaves loaf the skies,
I wonder if nameless monsters are in the sea,
I wonder if they are coming for me,
I wonder if wonderful wizards walk the skies,
Scary spiders with thousands of eyes,
Creatures of the darkness come to me, they are all scared I see,
Pesky pirates with popping eyes partying with a pal,
Prancing their pickles up and down.

**Olive Britland (10)**
St Joseph's Catholic Primary School, Newbury

# In A Trance

My dreams have been crushed,
I'm in a rush.
I'm getting to the end,
Please give me a lend!

My dreams have been crushed,
You have to hush!
I'm running out of time,
It's smaller than a dime.

This is the end,
I need a friend.
I have no hands,
And I have no plans.
Please give me a chance,
Before I'm stuck in this trance!

**Lilah O'Sullivan (9)**
St Joseph's Catholic Primary School, Newbury

# What A Fishy Dream, With Frogs Too!

Funny fish flop on thick fresh grass,
Fly far from Flipington into fluffy candyfloss,
For fuzzy wings appear for fish on Friday.

Flinging frogs far,
To finish first in the frog race,
While wearing fashionable fur coats,
Is fun for fish!

Finally they fry figs for a feast,
With frog friends,

Phew!

**Lily Polland (9)**
St Joseph's Catholic Primary School, Newbury

# The Future Footballer

I dreamed about myself as a footballer
My first football when you will be mine
One day I will be a football star
The captain of my team
My feet will perform a magical kick in the last minute
World Cup is in my hand.

**Noel Renson Kaduvinal (10)**
St Joseph's Catholic Primary School, Newbury

# Dream

**D** reams succeeded beyond their wildest adventure,
**R** emarkable dreams, remarkable days,
**E** verlasting dreams,
**A** lways keep dreaming,
**M** ade by dreaming and dream by making.

**Rutvi Verma (9)**
St Joseph's Catholic Primary School, Newbury

# Normal Candy Land

Probably just a dream. Then I checked my pocket... or was it?...
It began in a small old village. I looked around when I saw a light shine out from the wishing well. I looked closer to see what it was. As I looked deeper in the well the more tempted I got. So I got deeper, deeper and deeper and "Aarrgghh!" as I fell down the well. Luckily I landed on something soft. I looked at myself and I was a chicken! I looked beneath me and I saw... *marshmallows!* I didn't understand. So I bent down and picked one and "Mmmmmm!" it was the best marshmallow I ever had. So fluffy. Soft, squishy and sweet! I was filled with joy. I looked around and it was... *candy heaven!* The trees, green gumdrops, the clouds were cotton candy and the houses were cakes and ice creams! My mouth drooled when I saw this. So I was ecstatic and started stuffing my face with sweets, cakes and ice creams!
Suddenly, something weird started happening. There were headless chickens! I was so stunned and they started treating me like I was royalty! Started giving me sweets and a chicken coin. I stared at it as it glinted in the sunlight. I saw the same wishing well. I ran over and dropped the coin in. Then I was falling. I thumped in my bed.

**Kennesaw Arefi (10)**
Strand-On-The-Green Junior School, London

# Murder In The Dark

In a house, so big and tall,
Where shadows dance along the wall,
A mystery lurks, oh what a sight,
A crime happened in the dead of night.

Mr Bear was found on the floor,
His hat is gone, we can't ignore,
Detective Dog is on the case,
To solve the puzzle and win the race!

In the kitchen, Miss Kitty is there,
Singing a tune, but doesn't she care?
Her story's off, it doesn't fit,
Could she be the one involved a bit?

In the library, by the shelf,
A clue lies hidden, in itself,
A mystery grows, it's quite a sight,
Detective Dog walks through the night.

With magnifying glass in hand,
Detective Dog almost quit!
And then, in his brain,
With a suspect,
He *knows* who did *it*...

**Anais Kathrani (9)**
Strand-On-The-Green Junior School, London

# A Strange Amount Of Magic

In my dreams, when I lie in bed
The strangest stories fill my head
From fairies and monsters
To dragons and murderers
But one time, at night
This dream was particularly strange
It wasn't like a fairy tale, nor happy or light
It was dark and gloomy
And the chances of getting out were tight
The blood drooping down from the sky
Sprinted stealthily as the past went by
Suddenly, a character shot out
I was scared, like a cat. I pounced
It did a weird, peculiar ritual
I was afraid that staying here would be official
This neon green light was created
It opened its mouth and berated
"You're not escaping his prison.
With my power, you shall be risen."
Within a second, I was elevating
In the air, levitating

"Olivia, we're going out!" she shouted
That was all just a dream?
Oh, how crazy I can be!

**Suki Abdul-Jabar (9)**
Strand-On-The-Green Junior School, London

# Ships Love Cheese

When the clock strikes midnight
*Dong*
When everyone's asleep
*Zzzzzzz*
We'll take a peep inside your dreamy head
*Sshhhh*
We'll see if the dream dispenser is working
*Whiirrr*
And if it is, we'll take a look inside
*Eeekkk*
Pirate ships and asteroids floating through space
*Wow*
It gets weirder
*Bong*
The ships are eating cheese
*Munch*
We'll zoom into the ships
*Whoosh*
And ask them why they're eating cheese
*Why?*
The ships say
"I'm just hungry."
*Chomp*

"Would you like a ride?"
*Hhmm*
Well, you're going to find out next time
*Dun, dun, dun*
As it is time for school
*Briinngg!*

**Fredrik Blenkinsop (9)**
Strand-On-The-Green Junior School, London

# Shape-Shifter

In my dreams,
so big and wide,
wind whistles,
so pure and calm.

It's like I'm
in a whole new world,
ready to explore,
brave and strong.
Nothing scares me now...

I stretch my long and strong arm
up high in the air
to find out
I'm much shorter than before.

My hand is now a soft,
white and ginger paw;
my jaw is covered in fur.
I am a cat!
I walk, but now on all fours.

Then I'm a bird
that soars and flies.
My wings so thick and silky.
I'm flying so high
I'm almost touching the sun.

A soggy tongue licks me,
my dream now all gone.
It is my dog!
I'm late for school.

I can't wait to see
where my dreams
will take me next!

**Sophia Ball (10)**
Strand-On-The-Green Junior School, London

# Once Upon Hannah's Dream

In your dreams, anything could happen,
Whether it's dancing fairies or flying canaries,
Even deadly dinosaurs or mysterious monsters,
It could even be famous footballers or pesky pirates.

But tonight was different; tonight was scary,
Tonight there weren't dancing fairies or flying canaries,
But dragons!

Up in the sky, I could scarcely believe my eyes,
How could I escape its fearsome roars?
The monster swooped down from the sky like an eagle catching its prey.

It grabbed me with its lethal claws,
And it bared its razor-sharp jaws.

Menacingly, the wind howled around us,
The dragon was as fast as lightning and soared through the sky.

The beast lost its grip, and I fell onto my bedroom floor.

**Hannah Ferguson (10)**
Strand-On-The-Green Junior School, London

# The Cloud Of Cats And Frogs

Every night, my dreams take me away,
to a cloud where cats and frogs roam surrounded by hay.
The cats leave trails of pastel light,
while the frogs jump playfully in the night.

Usually, a deer-fox passes by,
hoping to take some food, or maybe spy.
Unfortunately, though, he just goes away,
I'd really like to see him stay.

I keep walking amongst the woolly blankets and piles of hay,
and see a cute frog called May.
She takes me to the witch's fire,
I watch them brew potions and doodle crazy spires.

Sadly, now it's time for me to go.
I see a kitten as she crouches down low,
and drags me away from this magical place,
and back into my bed, a cosy space.

**Carla Atkinson-Cruz (10)**
Strand-On-The-Green Junior School, London

# A Very Cattish Conversation

I've always wanted to talk to a cat,
And last night I had a dream I did.
It's funny that,
Dreams always feel so realistic,
But when you wake up it feels so far away,
Like a ball and you've hit it with a bat.
"Well, it would probably be more like a distant memory,
But I guess I could agree with that."
I looked over my shoulder,
And there YinYang sat,
Her purr rumbling like a diesel train.
"Oh, and hey, do you mind?
I'm currently having a bath,"
She said,
Daintily licking at her paw,
And,
Just like that,
She scampered off in a flash.
Something I've learned,
And I hope you have too,
Is that cats have a very,
Philosophical point of view.

**Marni Tang (10)**
Strand-On-The-Green Junior School, London

# Once Upon A Nightmare

Once upon a nightmare, clowns tag after me. They get their chainsaws ready in their hands, sprinting after me through a park. As I look back, I trip on squiggly tree roots that protrude through the ground. Adrenaline rushes through my body. I start to bleed through my nose, my ankles start to ache, and every muscle in my body tells me to stop, but I don't. I keep on running through the park, trying to keep my energy up.
I hide behind a tree, hoping they won't see me. They know where I am; I start running again; I tell my legs to hurry, but they don't. Faintly, I hear my mother's voice. Her voice gets clearer and clearer. Suddenly, I am starting to understand what she is saying.
"It's 7am! Time for school!"

**Aleksa Šegrt (9)**
Strand-On-The-Green Junior School, London

# The Vision In Front Of Me

Every night I go to sleep, I get this vision in front of me
The seas are blue, the land is red
Once was cool, now is not inside of this random place
Everything is weird
Kids tell adults what to do
People sleep in the morning and in the night the sky is bright
Animals can speak so can we
We eat grass, animals eat meat
Children work, adults go to school
On special days the sky is blue, normally it's the colour of goo
Dogs walk people in this world
Animals fly high - flying horses and my favourite, flying dinosaurs
Yes, in this world dinosaurs exist
They don't bite but may give a slight fright
I wake up and realise it's all out of sight.

**Anas Berkane (10)**
Strand-On-The-Green Junior School, London

# Dream Team!

I wish I had a dream,
A dream we had a team,
Two teams with a ball,
No hands. Yes feet. It's called football,
I don't play in goal but on the wing,
When I play football a million fans would sing,
I would win,
They'll nickname me King,
Ronaldo would assist,
So would IShowSpeed,
Messi would be messy,
So would Mr Beast,
The Rock would fight,
Tyson Fury on his side,
They'd be fighting and biting,
The opposition crying,
This was it, 90 minutes finished,
We got 8 goals, they got none,
I think it's simple. We won!
At the end, we drank beers
The other teams left in tears.

**Karter Escalante (10)**
Strand-On-The-Green Junior School, London

# Stuck In A Hug!

Everybody likes hugs,
However, how would you feel about being stuck in one?
A girl called Mia once went out with her friends,
They went shopping which was now a trend.
They saw a little boy who looked very sweet,
He gave a big smile and jumped up from his seat.
He went straight up to Mia's friend and hugged her,
Which was quite strange.
However, once he tried to let go, he couldn't.
What was going on?
Then Mia tried helping, then another friend,
Then another, but the hug would not end.
Finally... everyone fell to the floor.
They had done it, the hug was no more.

**Daisy Kent (10)**
Strand-On-The-Green Junior School, London

# Gym Bros

I went to one of my favourite gyms,
To work out all of my limbs,
And my hair needed trims.
I benched four-o-five,
And I met a guy named Clive,
We did dips and pushups,
Flips and more pushups.
We flexed in the mirror,
Ate chicken and liver,
And we planned to swim in the river.
We had our protein shake,
And thought of the friendship we could make,
We met The Rock,
And it blew off our socks,
We got a photograph,
And we had a good laugh,
In reps of fifty,
We felt so nifty,
And that's how I benched four-o-five,
And met a guy named Clive.

**Halel Braun (10)**
Strand-On-The-Green Junior School, London

# Random Dreams

In my dreams, I can see
Butterflies drinking tea.
Very funny, I know right?
But sometimes they do bite.
Nightmares are not my thing at all,
I can see spiders, oh, how they can crawl!
A bit scary, I know,
But they die from the snow.
Poor spiders dying,
They try to escape and I shout, "Keep trying!"
Now my happy dreams,
Happy and funny are my favourite themes.
So get prepared because they're still a bit funny,
The rivers are made of sweet honey.
And that's not it,
But I'm tired of this,
So goodbye and goodnight.

**Warisha Ghunidwal (10)**
Strand-On-The-Green Junior School, London

# Ancient Dinosaurs

In the days of long ago,
When giants roamed the Earth,
Stood creatures of immense size,
Known as dinosaurs, since birth.

Majestic beasts of ancient times,
Ruled the land with power and might,
Their enormous flames were so grand,
Cast a formidable sight.

With razor-sharp teeth and claws,
And scales as tough as stone,
They were kings of their domain,
And reigned supreme alone.

From the mighty T-rex,
To the peaceful brachiosaurus,
Each species had its place,
In the world's ancient chorus.

**Theresa Tian (9)**
Strand-On-The-Green Junior School, London

# Too Random For Me!

One day
In my dreams
I was at a weird bay
Full of steam
Then, up in the sky
Something flew down
It was a fly
A knife it took out of its pocket
It came out like a rocket
So sharp and bloody
While I was just muddy
I had my one strength
However, it was in my tent
I rushed to it
Oh so fast
There it was: my football kit
I took my football
And rushed over into a hall
There was the fly
I shot my football
Oh so high.

It disappeared,
No one ever saw it again,
Except me in my dreams.
## Eva Mark (10)
Strand-On-The-Green Junior School, London

# Once Upon An Animal

In my wonderful dreams at night,
Animals everywhere bright and colourful,
Patterns in shapes and mysticals,
Running like a cheetah, bright and early,
One by one, legs vanishing,
On the dusty ground they go,
The sharp claws and the long necks,
Further and further they go,
Colour like nothing before,
Further and larger they grow,
Grow down from Heaven,
Fur and skin they grow,
Every night they eat and sleep,
Hoping for no prey to come,
Sadly enough they stop right there,
For now, until they go next year...

**Kaysen Carter Cato (10)**
Strand-On-The-Green Junior School, London

# The Nightmare

This thing I couldn't bear,
I had a nightmare,
Where weird-looking aliens destroyed the world,
People were hypnotised,
Was not nice,
They killed, they hurt,
Buildings. Half were on the floor, same as the others,
Everything was torture.
But it was pure real,
And that wouldn't cure,
A healthy environment was turned into a nightmare,
Where?
Where was the amazing Earth I'm used to living?
It wasn't a mean world filled with sadness,
It used to be happiness,
But furiously it was, it was over!

**Maissa Callaki (10)**
Strand-On-The-Green Junior School, London

# The Olympic Stadium

There I was in the Olympic stadium while the crowd went wild. Almost everyone in the UK came just to see the Olympic stadium. Everyone - including me - was ready for the biggest finish of all. That was when me and the acrobats held each other's hands. Then we took a running start, and because we were so fast and put so much energy and so much strength, we threw ourselves high up in the air. In fact, I went so high up, I literally could touch the moon. And then the moment I touched the ground, I woke up from my sleep and then I thought it was like it really felt real.

**Drew Joshi (10)**
Strand-On-The-Green Junior School, London

# Rainbow Dreams

In a world of rainbow dreams,
Where colours dance and shimmer,
And hopes and wishes gleam.

A world so full of wonder,
Where skies are painted bright,
And every cloud is torn asunder.

In this place of pure delight,
Imagination takes flight,
And fills the night with light.

Dreams flourish and expand,
In the palm of our hands,
Guiding us to distant lands.

So let us close our eyes and believe,
In the magic that we weave,
In the realm of rainbow dreams.

**Nia Malhotra (10)**
Strand-On-The-Green Junior School, London

# Unicorns

Every night, I go to bed,
I have these thoughts inside my head,
I like to dream about unicorns,
The one that's silver with the spiky horns,
The one that gallops from roof to roof,
Collecting children's missing tooth,
They only come out during the night,
As they are scared, they might fright,
Their glossy mane glistens in the dark,
Then comes out a little spark,
I always hope they'll stay 'til day,
But they're always in their cave, waiting for prey.

**Tyler Kimpton (10)**
Strand-On-The-Green Junior School, London

# The Crazy Story/Poem

When I closed my eyes last night something didn't seem quite right
I spotted something outside in a tree
I was wondering what it could be
I couldn't believe what I was seeing
It was a human being
I crept over to have a closer look
I couldn't believe it... his hand was a hook
I could not believe my eyes
I think he was shy
I got closer
But I think I'm older
He said, "Hi,"
But I think I'm shy.

**Evie-Mae Stone (9)**
Strand-On-The-Green Junior School, London

# Dreams

I love dreams, what harm can they do?
You can dream about famous wizards or you can dream about you.
You can dream about flying football players or a dancing pirate.
And sometimes what you dream about can come true.
They go past you like a zoom or a flash of light and when you wake up, they will stay with you.
When you dream about space horses, they will twirl in front of you.
So when you dream, dream what you want and it will come true.

**Amelie Gray (10)**
Strand-On-The-Green Junior School, London

# Football Dream

In my dreams every night, footballs come bouncing from the sky.
I put the ball on the ground.
I kick. I score. I make the fans proud.
I lose the ball, my teammates go mad.
The other team scores, making our fans sad.
We reset and change the plan, so that we can come back.
The weather changed, and the rain poured.
We tried hard, and again we scored.
We celebrated until it was bright as a beam.
I woke up and realised the whole thing was a dream.

**Ranveer Seghal (9)**
Strand-On-The-Green Junior School, London

# The Secret Night Dream

In the dark of the night
Where I sleep
My visions come to life
I see the world in front of me
Where I fly on planets
I see the stars
Just like shining diamonds
I see the waves crashing together
Peaceful and quiet, I stay asleep
I see the animals right in front of me
I peacefully wake up from that joyful dream
I tell my friends and that dream is never
To be seen again
Goodbye for now.

**Grace Blissett (10)**
Strand-On-The-Green Junior School, London

# My Dreams

In my dreams all the time,
I think of a shining light,
Not so big,
Not so small,
But just perfect for us all,
Taylor Swift singing and dancing,
Footballers passing and laughing,
We all know we all have dreams,
But they are different for us each,
Some are scary,
Some are not,
Some go on,
Some just stop,
As I jump and cheer them on,
I feel like that's where I belong...

**Amia Akaye Taylor (10)**
Strand-On-The-Green Junior School, London

# Dreams Go As High As The Clouds

I'd dream I could fly,
Or reach the clouds up high,
Meanwhile wondering, is it true?
You could live in a world of your imagination,
Until it reaches your expectations,
Just like a mystery that you have to look into,
But now it is time for me to set off on my journey,
Which means I shall pause my hours of sleep,
I will always remember this dream,
Just until next time we meet.

**Meriam Grine (10)**
Strand-On-The-Green Junior School, London

# It's My Night

In my dreams, oh so bright,
I eat pizza, every night.
It's not my favourite food,
But it lightens my mood.
And that's one thing that I do every night.

In my dreams, oh my dreams,
I drive a Lamborghini,
Ferrari, Pagani.
And in my dreams, oh my dreams,
There is no school,
Instead, I play football,
Because it's my night.

**Marlowe Ward (9)**
Strand-On-The-Green Junior School, London

# Cosmic Astronaut

In cosmic realms, a lone soul takes flight,
To enchanted worlds, overlooked at night,
Amidst ancient ruins and creatures galore,
He braves the unknown, seeking more.

Through peril and challenges, his spirit prevails,
Unravelling mystery, as destiny hails,
A hero returns, his legend not failed,
In the silence of space, he shapes the world.

**George Price (10)**
Strand-On-The-Green Junior School, London

# A Fright In The Night!

In my dreams every night,
We all have a sight but,
Some may have more.

In my dream I had only one on that night, it was a fright,
It was a fight,
Still, none was right,
In the dark with no light,
There was a clue,
Though still people were blue,
Everyone knew,
But they stood back,
With a lack of patience.

**Lilia Ali (9)**
Strand-On-The-Green Junior School, London

# Beyblade

I am a blader,
My boy is the strongest,
I will burst the other Beys,
So I can win,
I have a strong bond with my Bey,
My favourite move is Astral Whip,
It will tear anyone apart,
My Bey's name is Spryzeh,
We will take on anyone and win.

**Muscab Abdikhader (10)**
Strand-On-The-Green Junior School, London

# Toaster

One night, I dreamt a toaster destroyed the school all with cheers and boos. Then the next thing I knew I was falling in a toaster slot. The bread came out and grew some legs. I was riding it to space. I look at my hands and I'm a velociraptor.
*What?!*

**Patrick Roche (10)**
Strand-On-The-Green Junior School, London

# My Grandfather

Most nights,
I find my head,
Dreaming about the person I love.
His hugs are as soft as a glove,
He's kind and caring,
And always loves sharing.
He loves to write poems,
Which are oh-so-charming,
Just like my grandfather!

**Jessica Hayward (10)**
Strand-On-The-Green Junior School, London

# Getting Lost

In my dream every night,
A man comes to my,
House all of a sudden,
*Bang, bang,*
I was in a forest,
I ran but too late,
I ran too far out,
Questioning myself,
Who am I?
Where am I?
And am I alive?

**Annabelle Carballo (10)**
Strand-On-The-Green Junior School, London

# When I Hold My Breath

When I hold my breath I fly
So very high
I touch the sky
To then fall but stop
Before I go *pop*
To wake from my slumber
And go to sleep again
Where I hold my breath
To go so very high
I touch the sky.

**Oscar Payne-Davis (10)**
Strand-On-The-Green Junior School, London

# Legendary Fire-Breather!

It was bedtime for me (Mike)
As my gorgeous mum tucked me into my secure, cosy bed
I slowly closed my sleep, exhausted eyes
I drifted off to sleep
It was time for my imagination to take me wandering!

As I teleported into my peculiar dream
I noticed something amazing!
I was in glimmering iron armour!
I was also equipped with a pointy, razor-sharp sword
Suddenly, I saw something: scaly, crimson-red
And with a malicious look in its eye
I was going to have to defeat this sinister creature!

As I charged with my courageous war cry,
The traumatising dragon breathed its sweltering fire.
I swiftly dodged it,
Suddenly, the dragon was wide-eyed,
As I pierced my razor-sharp sword through its robust chest!
I had saved the village
I woke up with joy!
And my cat was on the mat.

**Romeo Pira (11)**
Thomas Willingale School, Loughton

# My Beautiful Dream

I lie in the darkness,
My eyelids slowly dropping over my eyes like blankets.
Then my hazel eyes open again, seeing the same blue midnight sky.
I am sitting on cotton candy clouds so soft to the touch.
I see the moon staring down at me, a calming smile on her face.
I have wings that flutter like a fairy's.
I fly up to see bright lights that look like floating lanterns nestled in the sky,
I touch one and my finger glows silver.
Now glitter is made when I move it.
The glitter spirals around me and I magically get taken into a portal.
I open my eyes to see that I am in my warm bed,
A blanket draped over my body.
The curtains are drawn and Mum and Dad are smiling down at me.

**Celeste Cotrina-Vasquez (11)**
Thomas Willingale School, Loughton

# Once Upon A Dream

In a vision of the dark night,
I have a dream of joy departed,
But a walking dream of life and light,
Hath left me broken-hearted,
The Earth becomes a peaceful world,
Every animal becomes friends and no one complains,
I can see enjoyment on people's faces, I feel refreshed and delighted to be here,
The holy dream, that holy dream,
While all of the world were cheering,
They cheered for as a lovely beam,
A lonely spirit guiding,
I feel that I am in Dreamland,
Through that light, through that storm and night,
So tremble from afar,
What could there be,
More purely bright in truth's day star,
All that we see on streets is but a dream,
Within a dream.

**Salwa Inayat (10)**
Thomas Willingale School, Loughton

# The Creature Who Roamed The Night

It was a dark night,
Where there was no light,
There was no one around me,
Except for a creature behind the tree.

It gave me quite a fright,
I didn't believe I saw such a sight,
I turned away thinking it was an owl,
But then I heard a loud howl.

I found myself running away,
Since I knew I couldn't stay,
I thought it could dangerously bite,
So I ran with all my might.

I stopped and looked left and right,
It was out of sight,
I heard the footsteps behind me,
Whatever could it be?

I looked behind,
But all I could find,

Was the creature as black as a widow,
Suddenly it revealed itself from the shadow...

## Ella Leung (9)
Thomas Willingale School, Loughton

# Space Journey!

I was in my cosy bed, sleeping deep in my dream,
I was in a massive, ash-grey and garnet rocket with my brother,
As the rocket went zooming up into space,
Me and Romeo saw the ground fade so fast,
We only caught a glimpse of our house,
I heard the fiery engine roaring every second of the minute,
Me and Romeo cheered in delight as we saw the shiny, unreal, amazing, glistening stars up close,
We landed on a mysterious planet.

It was a dark, dull planet,
We explored the planet and it had deep holes,
As we place the flag on the planet, we smiled happily,
As we walked back to the rocket, we took our last look at everything,
Once upon an amazing dream.

**Maximo Pira (11)**
Thomas Willingale School, Loughton

# The Final!

Nerves bubbling, lights flashing, crowd roaring.
This is what I have always dreamed of.

A stadium, full of fans, expecting the win for their country.
Running down the line, ball at my feet.
2-1 down! Pressure's on!

Down in the penalty box, literally down.
Her studs hit me! Is this the end?

Whistle blows, Ref points at the penalty spot.
Can we equalise? Pressure's on!

Step up, deep breath, *swoosh!* Top bins!
That's the equaliser, crowd vaulting from their seats.

Half-time whistle blows, manager's face etched with worry; she turns pale.
There's a lot on the line!

**Evie-Paige Bohle (11)**
Thomas Willingale School, Loughton

# Dragons

**D** arkness covers me like an invisibility cloak as I'm nowhere to be found.
**R** oots sneakily watching, horror stricken as they dig back deep into the ground.
**A** s I creep steadily, the darkness engulfs me as I can no longer see,
**G** leaming lights coming from the heart of the forest are as powerful as a love potion. As I walk to it, my eyes gleam.
**O** minous sounds are heard as my mouth drops agape to see a dragon with scales shinier than a diamond.
**N** ervously, I cautiously walk towards it as I touch its rough, scaly wings as it lifts me in the air. I'm not scared because I no longer care.

**Jasmina Avdia (10)**
Thomas Willingale School, Loughton

# The One-Piece Dream

I'm the captain of this merry ship,
Come with me as I take you on a trip.

The swordsman finds the best spot to sleep on deck,
Don't challenge him, you will end up a wreck.

Raise the sails and take the helm,
We are going to get that crown.

The navigator shouts, "Listen to me,
Without my skills, we will be lost at sea."

The cook keeps us all well-fed,
Without him, we would have empty stomachs going to bed.

The sharpshooter bares a slingshot,
He mans the cannons ready for fight.

Off we go to the vast blue seas,
Off we go, my crew and me.

**Alano Reis (11)**
Thomas Willingale School, Loughton

# When I Dream...

When I dream, I dream of
Being a famous footballer scoring
The most incredible, memorable goal
And being a top midfielder
Like Joe Cole

When I dream, I dream of
Playing for West Ham
With moves so slick
When the ball comes to me
I give it a flick over my head
It's a goal!
A bicycle kick

When I dream, I dream of
Celebrating with my football team
I look in the distance
My fans are celebrating in excitement
I hear them all scream

When I dream, I dream of
Wearing claret and blue.
I hope that one day
My dream will come true.

**Harley Uren (10)**
Thomas Willingale School, Loughton

# The Jungle

This is a story of a sugar glider. Now we will begin.

There was once a sugar glider. He lived in the Amazon Rainforest. He was on a tree. He wanted to glide like all of the other sugar gliders but he was too scared. What he didn't know was that a snake was approaching him! He looked at the snake and jumped. He was gliding. He was so happy when he reached the ground. He had to go back to the tree because that was his home. So he did and the snake was not there. Where was the snake?

**Luca Winter (10)**
Thomas Willingale School, Loughton

# In The Kitchen

In the kitchen, pots and pans clang
While the essences make a flavourful dish with a delicious tang
From crispy trout to tasty pizza
Food is always a teaser

Carrots crunch and apples are sweet
A rainbow feast, a culinary treat
Whisking, stirring, flavours dance
In pots and pans, a culinary romance

*Sizzle, simmer*, the aroma blooms
In the kitchen, magic looms
With all the flavours melting
And food altogether smelting.

**Isobel Earl (10)**
Thomas Willingale School, Loughton

# Wonder A Dream

As I drift off to sleep,
A million dreams fly through my head.
Each one is different,
Which one is for me?

I could ride on the back of a unicorn,
Or explore a haunted house,
Slide down a mountain of acorns,
Get a new pet mouse,
And eat lots and lots of sweets!

My mum would say dream on,
If I told her all my dreams.
I wonder, I wonder,
If some dreams can actually come true.

**Rosie Bevan (11)**
Thomas Willingale School, Loughton

# My Trip Around The World

First, I went to France,
To see how they dance.

Second, I went to Greece,
To go and visit my niece.

After, I went to Spain,
To see the pretty plains.

Next, I went to Brazil,
To try and learn a new skill.

Last, I went to the Philippines,
To try their famous beans.

When I came back home,
I realised that everywhere
Is nice, but at home is the best.

**Diana Sojka (11)**
Thomas Willingale School, Loughton

## Seasons

Winter will turn into spring,
Spring will turn into summer,
Summer will turn into autumn,
And that's the seasons of the year.

Winter is snowy and icy,
Spring is warm and rainy,
Summer is hot and sunny,
And autumn is windy and cold.

Winter will turn into spring,
Spring will turn into summer,
Summer will turn into autumn,
And that's the seasons of the year.

**Mina Aparan (11)**
Thomas Willingale School, Loughton

# Not Just

It's not just about running,
It's mastering the skill to run faster.
It's not just about running past the finish line,
It's using all one's might to chase a dream

Faster than a lightning bolt,
Knowing one can become a national hero like Usain Bolt,
Or others in their lane, who came before, that had made an
Impression that outlasts their performance.

**Rida Oluwa (10)**
Thomas Willingale School, Loughton

# Flying Fairies

Fairies big and small gather round Pixie Dust Pond
They cheer and laugh
But there is always one fairy who has to ruin it all
No one knows his name
All they know is the devastation he causes
So every year they fly away to get away from the devastation
But legend has it, one of the fairies is brave enough to stay and fight...

**Ava Price (10)**
Thomas Willingale School, Loughton

# Dream

**D** aring dreams, dark and bright, some filled with colour and some filled with fright.
**R** eady to fight crazy knights.
**E** verybody has a dream and everybody has a fear.
**A** little dream can do a lot, it can inspire us to reach the top.
**M** any people like to dream of cars, houses and rocket beams.

**Iker Gutowski-Guerra (11)**
Thomas Willingale School, Loughton

# I Dream

I dream I had more pets,
I dream I could play Juliet on set,
I dream I spoke up more,
I dream I do well in the SATs,
I dream I was smarter,
He dreams he is rich,
He dreams he will never be bullied,
He dreams to be popular,
He dreams to be famous,
We dream!

**Milagros Zorrilla Grzelak (10)**
Thomas Willingale School, Loughton

# Make-Up Shop

**M** astery
**A** cknowledged
**K** indheartedness
**E** lectrodialysis
**U** ncommunicative
**P** rofessionalism.

**S** emidocumentary
**H** yperinsulinism
**O** rganometallic
**P** rofessionalism.

**Millie Pickard (11)**
Thomas Willingale School, Loughton

# Dream

Every child dreams of flying
Tell me, is it impossible?
Wings are given by Mom and Dad
Believe in children's strength!
Any dreams can come true
Steadily to the goal
Relative will support and help
If you want to fly - fly!

**Nadia Prokopchuk (11)**
Thomas Willingale School, Loughton

# Dreams Can Fly

Dreams are like wings on a bird,
Without them, you can't fly,
If you can't fly,
You can't live life,
Life is everything,
Life is you,
You are that bird, so fly high and dream big!

**Lurdes Griciute (11)**
Thomas Willingale School, Loughton

# YOUNG WRITERS INFORMATION

We hope you have enjoyed reading this book – and that you will continue to in the coming years.

If you're a young writer who enjoys reading and creative writing, or the parent of an enthusiastic poet or story writer, do visit our website www.youngwriters.co.uk. Here you will find free competitions, workshops and games, as well as recommended reads, a poetry glossary and our blog.

If you would like to order further copies of this book, or any of our other titles, then please give us a call or visit **www.youngwriters.co.uk**.

Young Writers
Remus House
Coltsfoot Drive
Peterborough
PE2 9BF
(01733) 890066
info@youngwriters.co.uk

**YoungWritersUK**  **YoungWritersCW**
**youngwriterscw**  **youngwriterscw**